Golden Legend of Young Saints

Other books by Henri Daniel-Rops
from Sophia Institute Press®:

Heroes of God

What Is the Bible?

Henri Daniel-Rops

Golden Legend of Young Saints

SOPHIA INSTITUTE PRESS®
Manchester, New Hampshire

Golden Legend of Young Saints is a translation of *Légende Dorée de Mes Filleuls* (Paris: La Colombe). The English edition was first published in 1960 by P. J. Kenedy and Sons, New York. This 2008 edition by Sophia Institute Press® includes minor revisions.

Sophia Institute Press®
Box 5284, Manchester, NH 03108
1-800-888-9344
www.sophiainstitute.com

Library of Congress Cataloging-in-Publication Data

Daniel-Rops, Henri, 1901-1965.
    Golden legend of young saints / Henri Daniel-Rops.
        p. cm.
    Originally published: New York : P.J. Kenedy, [1960].
    ISBN 978-1-933184-37-1 (pbk. : alk. paper) 1. Christian saints — Juvenile literature. I. Title.
    BX4653.D313 2008
    282.092′2 — dc22
    [B]
                                                        2008041303

08 09 10 11 12 13 9 8 7 6 5 4 3 2 1

Contents

∞

∞

The Golden Legend

The "Golden Legend" — a lovely name, but do we know what it means? In Europe, in those far-off days we call the Middle Ages, the title was a household word. It stood for an enormous book in which a learned priest had set down everything he could find about the saints and martyrs of the Church, everything he thought interesting, strange, amusing sometimes, and, of course, instructive.

Everywhere, in castle and monastery and township alike, people read or listened to the "Golden Legend," never wearying of its stories. How wonderful to hear of the miracles performed by Almighty God to help the saints in their labors! How thrilling to learn of the martyrs' exploits, of their bravery in the face of the most frightful torments! And how encouraging, after you had heard of the thousand and one tricks the Devil plays on men, to find that God always wins in the end, that Satan is always outwitted and put to flight!

Where did these stories come from? From all kinds of places and from the very earliest centuries. Think, for a moment, what the faithful must have talked about most in the first days of Christianity. Surely about what they cared for most dearly — Jesus, and Mary, His Mother, and His Apostles. About these beloved figures they could never learn enough, and since the Gospels are silent on many points, the faithful had to rely on the memories of people who themselves had witnessed or heard tell of this or that incident. And that is how so many marvelous tales came to be told and passed on from one person to another.

Or think, again, of the Christians who lived during the first persecutions. It needed plenty of courage, in those days, to declare openly that one had been baptized. Yet whenever the Roman emperors tried to stamp out Christianity, we find men, women, and even children preferring to suffer torture, to be burned alive or thrown to the wild beasts, rather than betray our Lord. So it is hardly surprising that the story of the mighty deeds of those heroes should have been cherished and told and repeated from generation to generation.

I cannot guarantee, of course, that everything in those wonderful stories is absolutely true — "Gospel truth," as we say. The good folk who related them may well have made some additions of their own, or been over-ready to believe in supposed miracles and extraordinary happenings they had not checked. Fact and legend, therefore, are often so closely interwoven as to be hard to tell apart. But however that may be, we will always find in the medieval "Golden Legend" great Christian lessons in faith, hope, and charity, a splendid love of God, and examples of the highest virtues. And that is just what the title means — a legend golden, sparkling, light-filled, peopled with figures who cast their glow upon us, and stand radiant with the glory of Paradise.

This dazzling parade of Christian holiness did not cease with the end of the Middle Ages. Countless saints, Christian heroes, martyrs even, have been raised up since whose names can be added to the glorious roster. Some, indeed, must be living right now. The Golden Legend continues to this day, and the lives of our most recent saints were often just as admirable as those of the first Christians. Some of them you will read of in this book, and I am sure you will not find them dull.

Here, then, is a selection I have made for you from the finest chapters of the eternal Golden Legend. Why these rather than others? Open the book, and you will see. Among this multitude of saints, many were young people — teenagers and even little children. "Valor does not wait on years," says a poet. To be a saint — that is, to live in the love of God, in absolute obedience to His commandments, to practice the noblest Christian virtues, and even to offer one's life in sacrifice — one does not have to be grown up. In many cases, indeed, children have given an example to grown-ups; little Blandina was one. This book, then, is a kind of portrait gallery of admirable young people — child saints, boys and girls who practiced exceptional virtues from a very early age, still others who played some part in certain important episodes of Christian history.

You remember the scene in the Gospels where Jesus cried, "Let the little children come to me!" Here are children who answered that call, who sought Him, found Him, and lived joyously in His love.

Henri Daniel-Rops

✑

The Golden Legend of Young Saints

∽

A Child Who Knew Jesus on Earth

It happened at Tiberias, that delightful little Galilean town with its palaces and palm trees and flat-roofed houses mirrored in the crystal waters of the loveliest of lakes. Every day children came to the lakeshore, to launch their toy boats on the ripples, to build sand castles — to play, that is, as children always play on beaches in every part of the world and in every age. Among them, there was one little boy who seemed different. For some months now, there had been a strange, thoughtful air about him scarcely to be expected of a six-year-old.

His name was Marcellus, a Latin name, although his parents were of purest Jewish stock and belonged, in fact, to the famous tribe of Benjamin. But his father had served with the Roman troops and had named the boy after one of his soldier comrades. Marcellus was raised like most other little boys of his time, with plenty of freedom. For instance, although he was so young, he often went off by himself, with only his little white goat as a companion, roaming the countryside until he reached one of the lovely meadows overlooking the lake. There he would spend hours picking flowers, watching the pink flamingos wheel and call in the vast blue sky. Or he would sing songs for himself that he never sang for others because no one else could have understood them.

3

One day, when he had gone to pick anemones — the lovely dark-red kind with purple centers that grew in certain rock crevices he had discovered — he met someone. He had just clambered on all fours to the top of a hillock, his more agile little goat springing up beside him, when he saw a man standing alone, perfectly still, only a few feet away. The man's arms were raised as in prayer, his face upturned toward Heaven. Marcellus stopped dead, staring at the stranger. Then the man lowered his head and his hands. At the same time, his eyes fell upon Marcellus, and he gazed at the boy in silence. What a glance!

Marcellus never told anyone about that meeting, not even his mother or father. He never told anyone what had happened when the stranger had beckoned to him to draw near, and he had obeyed. He never repeated what the stranger had said. But since that meeting, Marcellus had become mysteriously grave, as though some tremendous secret had been placed deep in his little heart, some image engraved there that absorbed all his thoughts.

Spring had come, the marvelous spring of Palestine, with its mild, early sun and its bird songs. The vine in flower scented the clear air, and you could hear the pigeons and turtledoves cooing in the sycamore trees.

And, of course, the boys were down at the lake again. But while the little ones paddled delightedly in the pleasantly warm water, the older ones spent their time talking. They seemed very excited. Could it be, as they had heard some of the older people say, that a prophet had appeared in Galilee? A prophet, yes, one of those strange, extraordinary men whom God had often sent to His people to warn them, to advise them, to console them — the boys had learned about these things at the synagogue school. Yet for hundreds of years now, there had been no sign of a prophet! Was this one clothed in animal skins? Had the Lord purified his lips with a burning coal? Or, like the great Elijah, did he course through the heavens in a chariot of fire? For these boys and girls, whose reading primer was the Bible, were thoroughly familiar with the history of their people.

Anyway, this man had definitely performed miracles. He had cured the mother of one of the lake fishermen whom they all knew — Simon, the one with the big ten-oared boat. And at nearby Capernaum, it was said that a Roman officer had begged him to save his servant who was dangerously ill, and the prophet had restored the man to health with a single word, without even seeing him. The children at the lake were burning with curiosity.

And so, when little Rebecca, who always knew everything — girls being even more curious than boys — ran down to the beach one morning calling, "He's there! I know he is! He's sitting with his friends in the field up there, where the lilies are. And he's talking," the children were not in the slightest doubt as to her meaning. Rising like a flock of sparrows, they raced up the rocky path Rebecca had pointed to.

Great crowds were gathered around the prophet, so that at first the children could not even catch a glimpse of Him. All they saw were great circles of men and women sitting on the ground. But in the total silence they could hear His voice. Snatches of phrases reached them: "Blessed are the poor, for theirs is the kingdom of heaven . . . Blessed are they who mourn, for they shall be comforted . . ."

That voice! Marcellus recognized it, and his heart seemed to miss a beat. The stranger — the man he had met where the anemones grew.

He had to see him again. Nothing would stop him. He began to press forward, squeezing through the rows of people seated on the grass. It was not easy, for although some of the people he disturbed said nothing because they were too busy listening, others thrust him rudely back. All the same, he managed to get close enough to be able actually to see the prophet. Yes, it was He! Marcellus elbowed his way between two husky farmers who were blocking his view, and was about to rush forward when two of the prophet's followers stopped him, pushed him aside, and chased him away.

At the same moment, the eyes he remembered so well met his, and the prophet smiled at the boy. Then, turning to His friends, the prophet motioned to them to release the child. "Let this little one come to me!"

The next minute Marcellus was at the prophet's side. Or rather, he was pressed against His breast. The prophet's arms were around him, and the deep voice sounded right in his ears, saying things he did not altogether understand but which made his heart glow: "Let the little children come to me, for of such is the kingdom of God. Amen, I say to you: unless you become as children, you shall not enter into Heaven . . . Whoever receives one such child as this in my name, receives me. And whoever receives me, receives not me but God who sent me."

∞

Marcellus was never to forget those wonderful moments when he had been lifted onto the great prophet's lap and embraced by Him. A dozen chattering women escorted him home, eager to tell his parents all that had happened, but the boy's only concern, then and thereafter, was to see the Master again.

Whenever he heard that Jesus — for now he had learned the prophet's name — was to be at one place or another, he hurried there too. Those who followed the Master soon became used to seeing the little six-year-old among them, as serious as a grown-up and listening with rapt attention to the long sermons. And Marcellus's mother began to come with him. Like the rest, she would sit on the grass and listen to Jesus.

That is how Marcellus came to be among the jostling crowds at the water's edge the day Jesus had jumped into Simon's boat and had Himself rowed a short distance from the shore so that He might address and teach the people. And Marcellus was there again the night of the terrible storm, when the whole village was out at the little pier awaiting the boats that had been caught in the open waters. That is how he came to see the prophet's friends pull to land and step out, pale and shaken, and heard them tell their extraordinary story. Their boat, it seemed, had already begun to ship water and was in danger of sinking when Jesus had risen and spoken to the storm, whereupon the wind had abated and the waves had grown calm.

And Marcellus was there again the day — but that was an even better story! The prophet, according to rumor, was going to deliver a particularly important sermon on the mountain slope on the other side of the lake, and thousands of people had come flocking to hear Him. In fact, the Master's friends had to help the people to be seated in orderly fashion.

Then Jesus spoke. Marcellus did not understand very much, but he didn't care; just to hear the prophet's voice made him intensely happy.

After some hours, Jesus said to His disciples: "I have pity on these people, for they have now been with me three days, and have nothing to eat."

One of the disciples called out to ask whether anyone had brought food along. No one answered . . . Why, yes, Marcellus did happen to have some pieces of bread and a few little fried fishes in the cloth satchel in which he carried his lunch when he went to school. He took them to the disciple.

Suddenly the crowd gasped. What had happened? At a single word of Jesus, Marcellus's poor rations had turned into hundreds and hundreds of loaves and fishes, enough to feed the whole multitude.

∞

A year went by. Then the people of the townships and villages bordering the lake learned that the prophet had gone away. It was said that He had left Galilee altogether. He had gone from lovely, green Galilee in order to teach the men of Judea, over there far to the south. Marcellus's heart was heavy with sorrow because he would no longer see his friend, no longer hear that warm, gentle voice.

But when spring returned, his parents announced that they were going up to Jerusalem for the great feast of Passover. They put the best saddle on the donkey, along with two wicker baskets filled with provisions, and set out. Marcellus and his mother rode, his father walking at their side, in a whole company of friends. And as they went, they sang splendid hymns about the Almighty, about the people with whom He had made His covenant, and about Jerusalem, the holiest of all cities.

They arrived at the Golden Gate early on the Sunday before the Passover, and immediately went in search of lodgings, which were not easy to find with so many people pouring into the city. Just as they were coming through an archway into a little square, they heard a great noise of voices, and they hurried to see what was going on.

"It is Jesus, the prophet from Galilee!"

That was enough for Marcellus. He slid down from the saddle and dived into the crowd, alternately elbowing and squeezing his way through, until he arrived at the very front of the crowd. It was indeed Jesus — Jesus riding on a donkey, like any peasant. But what strength, what majesty there was about Him! He was a prince, a king!

People were throwing green branches, large palms, and even their tunics and coats before the hoofs of the little beast. And Marcellus cried out with all his might, in his high, clear voice: "Long live the Son of David! Long live the Messiah! Hosanna! Glory to God!"

The Master looked at him again, and the child knew He recognized him. But he could not get closer, for a group of bearded, long-haired men, their locks hanging far down upon their dark tunics, had rushed up to Jesus. They seemed to be angry about something. But never mind; Marcellus had found his friend again, and he was happy.

All that week, Marcellus kept trying to find the Master again, and several times he succeeded. One evening, as he was looking for Him in one of the less-frequented parts of the city, he met two men whom he recognized; they were disciples of Jesus. Marcellus was anything but shy. Going up to them boldly, he said: "I know you; you are the prophet's friends, aren't you? Well, I am His friend, too, and I want to follow Him."

One of the men looked at him closely and asked, "Isn't this the child the Master embraced?"

"Yes!" Marcellus cried. "It was I! It was I! Where is He? I want to see Him again!"

"Very well," said one of the men, "come with us, and you will see Him."

That was how Marcellus came to help Simon Peter and John prepare the room where the Master was to celebrate the Passover. And that was how he even had the privilege of serving with those who carried in the dishes at the Passover meal.

Standing in a corner of the room, whence he could see everything that was happening, he saw Jesus raise bread toward Heaven, then a cup of wine, and heard Him utter strange and beautiful words. And when Jesus asked for water and a towel, it was Marcellus, nimbler than the rest, who raced off to bring Him what He wanted.

Then Marcellus saw Jesus bend down, kneel almost, before each of his friends in turn, and wash their feet with His own hands. It was a custom the boy knew well, having often seen his father wash the feet of important guests. But what seemed strange to him was that so great a personage should observe the custom too, a prophet of whom it was even said that He was the Son of God.

∞

Would you like to know what became of that privileged child whose heart burned with love of Christ so early and so brightly? The poets of medieval France loved to relate this story:

After Christ's death and glorious Resurrection, Marcellus asked Simon Peter, the leader of the disciples, for baptism. Then, for a dozen years or more, he followed the great Apostle in all his missionary labors, until one day, St. Peter said to him, "There is a country far, far away called Gaul, where people have not yet heard about Jesus. You will go to that country. You will go to bring the Good News to the people who live there. I will give you two companions as helpers, but I shall also ask the Almighty to give you twelve angels to assist you."

Marcellus sailed for Gaul[1] and, upon landing, went on to a great city now known as Limoges. He has been its patron saint ever since, because he it was who brought the gospel there. Who knows? Perhaps the poets' tale is true?

---

[1] Roman Gaul was later overrun by the Franks, whence its present name.

∞

The Boy Who Fled in the Night

A sound broke the stillness of the night, startling the boy out of his sleep. What could it have been? Not the familiar roar of the brook called the Cedron, swollen now, in spring, its muddy waters churning and frothing over the pebbles close by the house. Nor the regular cry of the sentries on night watch on the ramparts of Jerusalem, calling out the password every fifteen minutes. Then what was it? Things were usually so quiet here, in this out-of-the-way spot on the city's edge. The boy jumped up from his bed — a reed pallet covered by a mat — and ran to the window.

His name was Mark. He was fifteen years old, and he lived alone with his widowed mother, Mary, on a property richly planted with olive groves. Here, to provide them with a modest income, Mary had set up an oil press to which the people of the neighborhood brought their olive harvests. That is why the property was generally known as Gethsemane, or "oil press."

But no one could be wanting to use the press at this hour! Mark leaned out of the window, searching the pale night. The full moon rode peacefully in the pearly sky, showing up the powerful fortifications and above them the majestic temple. The suspicious sound came from the steep path that ran down from the gate to the ford across the stream, a sound of voices, of clattering arms, of heavy boots ringing on pebbles. Mark could see the glimmer of torches piercing the shadows. His heart beat more violently.

Suddenly he had guessed. The band of men hurrying down the hill — he had guessed their sorry mission. He thought of his great friend and his friend's companions. They would be sleeping now, unsuspecting, beneath the olive trees in the garden, as they had asked his mother's permission to do. They must be warned! He was in such a hurry, he did not even trouble to dress; he picked up the sheet that had fallen to the floor and wrapped it around him like a Roman toga, then jumped from the low window into the garden below.

But he was too late. Before he could reach the Galileans, the soldiers and police had already surrounded that part of the olive grove. Mark hid behind a tree and watched, in utter anguish. He knew, of course, that the leaders of the people wanted to have the wonderful prophet arrested, but he could not understand why. What had Jesus done?

Mark had been following Him for the past six months along the roads of Judea; he could vouch for it that He had done nothing wrong. Jesus had healed the sick, restored sight to the blind, given generous alms to the poor, consoled the suffering. Were these the crimes He was reproached with?

The boy's heart revolted against the injustice of it. He would have liked to hurl himself at those ruffians, sword in hand, and scatter the whole miserable gang.

The reddish glow of the torches lit up the scene for him. He heard his friend's voice ring through the night, strangely calm: "Whom are you looking for?"

"Jesus of Nazareth!" — that was one of the temple police.

"I have told you that I am He. If you want me, let these go their way."

At that moment, the torchlight fell upon Jesus' face, and Mark was shattered at what he saw: a mask, as it were, of such suffering and agony that drops of blood seemed to glisten upon the skin.

Suddenly a violent commotion broke out. One of Jesus' companions, the eldest, had drawn his sword and struck a guard, who was now howling with pain, his hand on his ear. Again that voice rang out, so beautiful, so calm, this time addressing Peter: "Put up your sword into its place, Peter. Do you not know that I can ask my Father in Heaven, and He will give me more than twelve legions of angels? But is it not said in the Holy Scriptures that I must die for the salvation of men?" And, touching the soldier's ear, He healed him. Then, without a word, He held out His wrists to the guards and let Himself be bound.

It was unbearable! Mark was so stirred, so completely carried away by the horror of it, that without realizing it, he had come out of his hiding place in order to see and hear better, and was now standing in full view of the guards. Jesus' companions, taking advantage of the confusion that had just occurred, had fled.

"Well, we've got this one, anyway," cried a guard, throwing himself at the boy. Without a moment's thought, Mark fought back and managed to free himself. But in the scuffle, the sheet around his body came loose, and he tripped. He let himself fall to the ground, then jumped up again and raced off. The man was left holding nothing but a piece of cloth. Mark, meanwhile, darted off from olive tree to olive tree, swift as a young goat, and disappeared into the night.

∞

Mark went on running for quite a time. Were they following him? No, there was no sound either of footsteps or of arms. Light-footed as he was at his age, he must have outdistanced those brutes. But it would not be wise to go straight home; at the same time, the night was cold, and he was practically naked.

For a short while, he hid in the mouth of one of the tombs hewn out of the rock of the hillside, listening, looking. He could see quite plainly the glimmer of torches moving up the path that led back to the city, then disappearing through the gate of Jerusalem. Cautiously, and still very much on the alert, Mark returned to Gethsemane.

His mother was up, and several of her friends had joined her. Like her, these holy women had been disciples of Christ for some months, following Him everywhere, ministering to Him. Now, crushed by the cruelty and horror of what had just taken place, they were weeping. Jesus, their friend, their Master, in the hands of His enemies! He was lost. Who could tell what frightful fate awaited Him?

Mark told them what he had seen, and how he had got away himself. "But now," he cried, "I won't leave Him alone! The men ran away, and I'm only a boy, but I'll go up there, and I'll find Him! Maybe I'll even be able to help Him escape!"

Hurriedly he changed into the simple gray tunic worn by most boys of his age, and ran off up the steep path leading to the ramparts.

It did not take him long to guess where Jesus was: in the palace of the chief priest, Caiphas. For rumor had it that it was Caiphas who desired Jesus' death. Mark slipped into the courtyard. The servants and soldiers had lighted a fire there and were gathered around the blaze, warming themselves and discussing the affair.

Just as the boy joined the circle — no one paid any attention to him — an argument broke out. A woman cried out in a shrill voice, "You, too, were with Jesus of Nazareth!" She was pointing at a bearded man whom Mark recognized as Simon Peter, the man

Jesus had named chief of His disciples. Poor Peter! Of course he would admit it, and the guards would arrest him, too —

But instead, in a voice that shook (was it with rage or with fear?), Peter answered, "Woman, I do not know Him!"

Mark was thunderstruck. So even the best of the Master's friends was deserting Him! Then astonishment gave way to indignation, and he knew what he would do. Since the grown men were not capable of proclaiming their faith and sacrificing themselves for their leader, he, a lad of fifteen, would bear witness to Christ, whatever the cost to himself.

At that moment, Jesus left Caiphas's audience chamber and appeared on the threshold. Peter was still protesting, cursing and swearing, "I swear, I do not know what you are talking about!" The Master's eyes met Peter's, full of pity and wordless reproach, and the apostle was silent and hung his head. Then the escort brutally dragged the condemned man away. And Mark, mingling with the band of the curious, the guards, and the temple servants, set out after Him.

∞

He saw everything. He was in the crowd that waited several hours outside Pilate's fortified palace while the Roman governor questioned Jesus. He was right in the front of the crowd when Jesus was shown to the people, wretched, exhausted, barely able to stand, His features convulsed. His body all bloody from the scourging.

When his Lord was being led to the place where He was to be crucified, Mark kept coming as near to Him as he could. And several times the Master's eyes rested on him, with an extraordinary gaze that seemed to go right through him, to reflect some terrible, mysterious thing. Mark felt sure that with this look Jesus was calling him, that he, too, one day, would have to bear witness, that his true vocation from now on was to serve the Master even beyond the grave.

Mark was so tired that night when he came home to Gethsemane that his legs could scarcely carry him. His eyes were still full of the horror of what he had seen. The two hands nailed to the beam of the Cross, the blood flowing in long streams, the twisted body . . . and the astonishing, terrifying darkness, like a cloud of death, which had descended over the region as the Master entered His agony.

At Gethsemane, Mark found his mother in tears. She knew, and her heart, like his, was torn with anguish. Mark embraced her again and again. Then suddenly he drew himself up. What inner voice was dictating these words to him?

"Don't cry, Mother," he begged. "Don't you remember that Jesus Himself foretold all these things? And don't you know that He promised to rise from the dead?"

The boy went on talking late into the night, restoring his mother's courage. He reminded her how Christ had warned them of all that was to come. Since His prophecies had come true so far, should they not believe Him as to the rest? He would rise on the third day. They would see Him again alive, hear Him speak to those who loved Him. "On Sunday morning, at daybreak, we must go up to the tomb. Jesus can neither be deceived nor deceive others. I tell you, I know He will be alive!"

∞

Fifty days had passed since that night of anguish. Jesus had indeed risen. On Easter morning, Mark had seen his mother running home almost speechless with wonder. "The tomb is empty! He isn't there. I saw an angel — he was like a living light that spoke.

He told us that Jesus had truly risen. Ah, my son, my child, how great are the things of which we are the unworthy witnesses! All your life you must remember them. You, too, will have your task to fulfill for the divine Master."

Mark had seen Him, seen Him with his own eyes. He had been with the disciples the day Thomas had declared he could not believe in such extraordinary tales, and Jesus had appeared before him, saying, "Put your hands in my wounds, touch my side . . ." And Mark had witnessed, too, the supreme miracle on the hill right above his home: Christ mysteriously rising up to Heaven, to sit at the right hand of the Father. From that time forward, his faith was so firm that it never wavered.

Jesus had told His own, before He left them: "Go into the whole world, and preach the Good News to all men." Mark, in his own special way, would be a bearer of the Good News. Every day he joined the group of Jesus' friends who gathered to talk about Him, to recall His words, to live united as brothers.

Now, the fiftieth day was a great feast — Pentecost — in memory of the day Moses proclaimed the Ten Commandments from Mount Sinai. On that day, Christ's followers were assembled in one room when they heard a sound as of a mighty wind approaching and bursting into the very house where they were gathered. Then, what seemed like a ball of fire exploded, and tongues of flame scattered through the air, coming to rest on the heads of all the persons present there. They understood then that the Holy Spirit had just manifested Himself, and that He would thenceforth fill them all with His power. And immediately there occurred an even stranger thing: all of those there began to speak in different languages. They knew the languages without having learned them, obviously because the Lord wanted them to be understood by all the peoples to whom they would bring the Good

News. And the young boy Mark also felt extraordinary strength rising up in his soul; henceforth, he knew, he would have enough courage to consecrate his life to Christ.

∞

A crowd had formed outside the house where such a great prodigy had taken place. And upon hearing Christ's friends speak all those strange languages, the people began to say to each other: "They are drunk! They've been taking too much sweet wine!" But then Peter arose. He got up on a bench and started to address the crowd. Now he was not afraid! Now there was no thought of denying that he belonged to the Lord. This is what he said:

> Men of Judea, and all you who live in Jerusalem, I must tell you: We are not drunk, as you suppose, but the Spirit of God has come down on us and given us these mysterious powers. Now we must cry out the truth, and the truth is this: Jesus of Nazareth, whom you put to death in your wickedness, was the Messiah, the Savior of men. For centuries and centuries His coming was foretold by the prophets. It was promised that He would be born and would die and that all those who called on His name would be saved. And again I tell you: He has risen from the dead. Of this we were all witnesses, we who have called ourselves His followers. And, as He promised, His message will henceforth conquer the world and will spread through all the nations.

What courage! Mark was filled with admiration now; could he but serve these men in their glorious work of bearing witness to Christ! Oh, to give himself to Christ and His Good News!

When Peter stepped aside, the boy followed him. "I want to join you," he cried. "I want to labor in the Master's cause too!"

Peter looked at him, and affectionately laid his hand on Mark's shoulder. "I tell you, in the Lord's name, that you, too, my child, shall enter His service. You will have your part to play in the great task that awaits us all. And one day, the Master will ask of you the supreme sacrifice — to die for Him. Are you prepared for that?"

"I am ready," replied Mark firmly. And that is how the lad of the Garden of Olives became one of the first members of the Christian community. Later, when he was about forty years old, he wrote the Gospel that bears his name. And later still, at Alexandria in Egypt, where he had gone to preach the Good News, he died a martyr, for Christ.

On the Road to Damascus

Rabbi Gamaliel gave the signal for dismissal and was silent. The class was over. The dozen or so youths around him got to their feet, stretched, and began talking noisily. After nearly three hours of sitting cross-legged, tailor fashion, on their little mats, drinking in their teacher's every word, they certainly deserved some exercise. They were young fellows, between sixteen and eighteen. They wore the dark garments, unrelieved by any decoration, which marked them as Pharisees, the strictest of the Jews. And from their clothes there hung what looked like little boxes containing thin rolls of parchment inscribed with verses from the Law of God.

The Law of God! That was what they studied all day and every day with unwearying attention. In those days, books were little used in teaching, and students had to rely largely on their memories. "A good pupil," so the saying went, "is like a cistern without cracks; he loses nothing of what his master has poured into him." And so, early and late, for years on end, the future "rabbis" or "doctors of the Law" would listen to their master as he read out passages from Holy Scripture. Then they commented on them by quoting what the ancients had said about the same texts.

They learned the story of the patriarchs and of the kings; they chanted the psalms together; they searched eagerly in the marvelous writings of the prophets for passages announcing the coming of the Savior of the world, the glorious King who would deliver Israel from its wretched lot, the Messiah. And when Rabbi Gamaliel finished speaking — how well he spoke, how learned he was! — each of the students had to repeat the master's words to himself, so that he might be able to speak them out loud in his turn.

By twos and threes, they left the temple court with its huge portico beneath which they had been sitting. Then they went their separate ways through Jerusalem, up and down the narrow, sloping streets cut here and there by flights of steps. But one of them remained alone. For a few moments, he appeared to be thinking deeply. Then he, too, left the court, but instead of going down into the city, he made for the fortified gate and the country beyond.

How old was he? It was hard to tell. His face was already so grave, so worn for a young man. He was not handsome: of medium height, thick-set, bandy-legged, haggard, his red hair thinning on his head. Yet anyone looking at his face, with the bushy eyebrows meeting over the hooked nose, and the very lively eyes, would know that here was a young man of exceptional intelligence. He had come all the way from his native Tarsus, in Cilicia, to study to be a rabbi. In the two years he had been in Jerusalem, no pupil of Rabbi Gamaliel had worked harder, or more attentively, or with greater zeal to learn and understand. This young man, who always kept to himself, was named Saul.

∞

He had just left the city and was walking to an olive grove where he wanted to lie down in order to think and to go over the day's lesson, when the sound of shouting made him turn around. A mob was pouring out of the city gate, yelling, waving their arms, frenzied. In their midst was a tall, thin young man, carrying himself with extraordinary calm and self-assurance. Saul saw him, and he was filled with rage and hate.

Another of those people! Wasn't it enough that their famous prophet had been put to death? And what a shameful death! Six years ago, all Jerusalem could see Him hanging on a Cross, like a thief and a murderer, yet there they were, still repeating their fables. That miserable Galilean, that laborer's son, they claimed, was the Messiah. A glorious king indeed! Naturally, they had all sorts of trumped-up stories to support their claim. They said, for instance, that the impostor had come out of the tomb in which He had been laid, that He had risen, that He had been seen alive for forty whole days . . . Saul had not been in Jerusalem at the time, but the wise rabbis had explained to him why this Jesus could not possibly have been the Messiah, and why the chief priests and leaders of the people had been right to get rid of Him. What would happen to their holy religion if every madman was allowed to speak and act at his whim?

Saul drew nearer. He recognized the young man imprisoned by the mob — a fellow named Stephen, from Egypt probably, judging by his clothes. No, this was too much! Why were they allowing him to speak to them? He seemed strangely sure of himself, that lad. What was that he was saying? It was a long speech. Still the same absurdities? No, he was speaking of Abraham, of Moses, of the prophets. Oh, the liar! He had simply been leading up to the statement that Jesus had really been the promised Messiah, the Savior of Israel. Fraud! Fraud!

"There was not one of the prophets your fathers did not persecute. They killed all those who foretold the coming of the Just One, whom you in these times have betrayed and murdered; you, who have received the Law from the hands of angels and have not kept it."

"He's insulting us! He's making fools of us!" Saul cried out as loudly as he could.

"Put him to death!" yelled the mob, and again, "Put him to death!"

Whereupon, without so much as an attempt at a trial, they pushed Stephen into a corner of the city wall, threw him down, and made ready to murder him.

"You there!" called one of the men, throwing his tunic to Saul. "Keep our clothes while we settle with him!"

And while the stones hailed down upon the unfortunate young man, Saul watched, unable to tear away his eyes, his jaws clenched in a strange rage. Stephen remained as self-possessed as ever.

"So you see him, that Messiah of yours?" yelled one of the murderers as he aimed a big stone at him.

"I see the heavens opened," replied Stephen, "and the Son of Man standing on the right hand of God."

At that moment, the heavy stone struck him on the temple, and he fell. They could hear him stammer a few more words: "Lord, do not count this sin against them." Then he lay still. He was dead.

∞

Saul could never forget that scene. For days on end, he could not put it out of his mind. Try as he would, he could not get over the young man's calmness. What madness to suffer death for the sake of a poor impostor, a failure, a laughingstock! Yet when he thought of that splendid face turned heavenward in prayer, when he remembered Stephen's look as their eyes had met for a moment — and how strangely penetrating it had seemed — he was hard put to it to stifle his uneasiness.

On the Road to Damascus

Suppose, after all, those people were right? Suppose Jesus really had been the Messiah? No, no, it simply was not possible. All of Holy Scripture was against such an absurd notion. The rabbis had proved that over and over again. And yet in the writings of some of the prophets — Isaiah was one, and he was perhaps the greatest of them all — were there not also some singular passages that seemed to suggest that the Messiah would suffer and die to redeem mankind?

Thoughts like these jostled each other in Saul's mind, driving him nearly distracted. As a matter of fact, since he had seen Stephen die, he had altogether lost his peace of mind. A kind of fury kept boiling up in him, against himself, against others, and especially against all who were friends and followers of the Crucified. So he began to scour the city for "Galileans," and as soon as he found any, he would hasten to the leaders of the people, to the grand council known as the Sanhedrin, to have them arrested. Men, women, children — all were objects of his fury. But this activity did not make him any happier or more peaceful than before. On the contrary, his inner torment grew with every day that passed.

One day, one of the members of the council said to him, "Those Galileans are all over the place now, not just in Jerusalem. They are like the plague — they spread. You are so good at tracking them down, Saul, why don't you go to some of the other cities to warn the leaders of our people of the danger and have those fanatics arrested? Start with Damascus, in Syria. It seems there are quite a number there. Good hunting, my boy!"

∞

For a whole week, Saul had been trudging along the sandy road that led from Jerusalem to Damascus. The green valley of the Upper Jordan was behind him, and before him stretched the barren plain with its dry grasses crackling in the wind. To the left, Mount Hermon reared its snow-capped peak into the steely blue sky. It was a beautiful summer day, sultry as summer days so often are in Asia, and close to noon.

Saul was in a hurry to arrive in Damascus, to throw himself into the police job entrusted to him, to lay his hands on those people he hated. His fury was mounting with every step he took along his solitary way. To prove to himself that he was right, he must see to it that those stupid madmen were arrested, imprisoned, perhaps even killed . . .

All of a sudden, a light shone out of the sky, enveloping him in its brightness. No, it was not the sun — it was a strange light, whiter than lightning, more terrible, more penetrating. Before he could realize what was happening, he found himself lying flat on the ground, incapable of the slightest movement.

At the same moment, a voice sounded in the immense silence of the plain. "Saul, Saul, why do you persecute me?"

Without even wanting to, he heard himself choke out the question: "Who are you, Lord?"

And the voice replied: "I am Jesus, whom you persecute."

For Saul, this was a moment of utter consternation. He was defeated, crushed, yet he wanted to rebel again, to stand up to that mysterious force.

But again the voice sounded in his ears, at once so firm and so sweet, charged with mercy and consolation: "It is hard for you to kick against the goad."

So the invisible power knew everything! He could read the inmost secrets of the soul!

Trembling, Saul murmured, "Lord, what will you have me do?"

And the voice replied, "Arise, and go into the city, and there you will be told what you must do."

There could be no more argument. The young man got up reeling, then uttered a cry of despair. Instead of the blazing noonday sun, there was complete darkness — his eyes were open, but he could see nothing.

At that moment, some horsemen drew near. They stopped and asked him why he was shouting like that, all alone at the side of the road, covered with dust and with his arms outstretched. Had robbers waylaid him? It seemed to them that they had heard the sound of voices, but they had not been able to make out the words and had seen no one. They did not understand.

But Saul, for his part, had understood.

Slowly, a blind man now, he set out again and arrived in the city. Beyond the massive tower guarding the city gate, there stretched a broad avenue called Straight Street leading to a pagan temple. Saul followed the porticos bordering the avenue. He had been given the address of a Jew named Judas, a merchant established at Damascus on business and a friend of the Pharisees. Judas was to give Saul hospitality and help him in his task of tracking down the Galileans.

But it was no zealous prosecutor of the followers of Christ whom Judas welcomed to his house. It was a wretched blind man who sat down in a corner of the room and remained sitting for days, silent, distraught, his eyes open upon a perpetual night, the night of his punishment. He refused all food. He would not answer any questions about his strange experience. Crushed, devastated, the youth seemed now more like a man of sixty.

He had understood. Jesus, whose voice had sounded in his ears on the sun-baked road, was punishing him, and it was only just. He it was who had made Saul blind, and what good would it do to rebel? All Saul's past cruelties, all the bitterness in his soul, all these were pouring down on him now and plunging him in this darkness. It was only fair. He knew it, and he accepted the penalty. But at the same time, he felt sure that Jesus would not punish him forever, that He would have pity on him, that He would spare him. Over and over again, in the dreams that flitted through his darkness, he seemed to see a man with a very kindly face leaning over him, placing the palms of his hands on Saul's eyelids, and then . . .

One day, a man came to Judas's door asking whether a blind traveler had not recently arrived there from Jerusalem. The master of the house gave him a cold welcome; he knew Ananias was one of those fanatics who followed Jesus. But he could not really refuse to answer the man's question, so finally he led him in to his guest.

"Saul," said the visitor, "rise up!"

At the sound of his voice, the blind man turned his head.

"Listen to me, Saul," said Ananias. "In a dream I saw my Lord and Master, Christ Jesus, and heard His voice. He told me to go to Judas's house in Straight Street to find a young man who had need of me. He told me your name and said I was to lay my hands on you, so that you would be cured of blindness. Brother Saul, I have come . . . yet I know who you are. I dared tell my Lord that you are known as one of the worst enemies of His people, of all the harm you have done to His saints in Jerusalem. But one does not disobey the voice of the Master, so I am here."

"No, Ananias, one does not disobey the voice of the Master," Saul murmured.

Then Ananias laid the palm of his hand on Saul's eyelids, and the young man's sight was restored. He rose up and was baptized.

∞

You know what became of that young man, Saul, to whom these astonishing things happened. As Paul, a name he took later, he became one of the Church's greatest saints. He it was who founded the first great Christian missions in pagan countries; he it was who carried the Good News heroically, for years on end, throughout Asia Minor, Greece, and Italy. He was a great writer too, and his marvelous letters — the Epistles — have done so much to make known Christ's teachings. Finally, in the course of Nero's brutal persecution of the Christians, Paul, in Rome, died for Jesus, beheaded by the axe of the executioner. Blessed Paul, whose violence and fury had been but the symbols of his greater hope! Blessed Paul, so loved by Jesus that He had pierced his heart on the road to Damascus!

∞

Beautiful St. Agnes

Daybreak over Rome. Heavy boots ringing on the paving stones. Violent knocking at the door. "Open!" Soldiers storming in, sword in hand, ready to strike anyone offering resistance. But those they came to arrest had no intention of resisting. They had accepted their fate in advance; they had already given their lives to Christ.

They would not deny their Lord. Led before the imperial judge, they faced him without tremor. There followed an exchange more or less like this:

"Are you a Christian?"

"Yes, I am."

"Will you sacrifice to the gods of Rome?"

"I cannot."

"If you refuse, you will die."

"I refuse."

This dialogue was repeated not dozens but hundreds of times. Countless were the men, the women, the children who, before the imperial authorities, proudly proclaimed their faith in Jesus Christ and chose to die rather than betray Him. These "passions," these sublime stories of sacrifice accepted, longed for, by generations of Christians, form what is probably the most admirable chapter in the history of the Church.

The early Christian martyrs! Were they not witnesses for Christ? In Greek, the word *martyr* means "witness." Were they not living proofs that, for Christians, fidelity to the baptismal promises is more important than life itself? Century after century, their names were to be remembered, their stories repeated, their intercession invoked.

There were many children in this glorious band of martyrs, just as brave as their elders, displaying the same flawless heroism in the face of the most frightful torments. And what torments! For the pagan Romans inflicted almost unbelievable cruelties on the Christians.

Can you imagine how boys or girls of thirteen or fourteen must have felt when they were bound to a stake, coated with pitch, and when they saw the executioner draw near with the torch that was to set them on fire? Or in the circus, as the youthful martyrs watched the bars suddenly lifted and a troop of ravenous lions, leopards, and bears descending upon them? That those little Christians should have had the strength to remain faithful — that is the eternal, the admirable mystery. Without any doubt, Christ Himself must have given them of His own strength at the moment of their agony, must have been invisibly present to assist them.

St. Agnes was one of those child martyrs whose lovely story never loses its attraction. She was thirteen and very beautiful; indeed, more than beautiful. The soft light of her eyes, the perfection of her features, and the natural grace of her body were matched by an angelic charm, a transparency of soul, that made her stand out among all her companions. Her name signified "the most pure," and she deserved it certainly.

Her parents were of the nobility and very wealthy, and they gave her an education worthy of her rank. Agnes, for her part, attracted attention from her earliest childhood by the ease with which she understood and learned whatever she was taught. But what she wanted to learn most of all, far more than the knowledge contained in books, were the virtues leading to holiness.

Often she would be absorbed in prayer for hours on end, sunk in deepest contemplation — in what is called ecstasy — where nothing existed for her but her love of Christ. And often, during those extraordinary moments when her soul seemed to leave the earth and soar directly to Heaven, she felt certain that Jesus Himself had come to her, had spoken to her, had promised to accept her among His chosen, and that He returned the love she had given Him so completely.

Every day, as she walked home from school, a young man would meet her on the way. He was the son of the pagan governor of Rome, a fine lad of eighteen or twenty, full of vigor and spirit. Agnes looked much older than she was; she carried herself so nobly and she was so beautiful that the boy fell in love with her. One day, therefore, he came to her parents' house and begged Agnes to be his wife.

It was an awkward moment. To say no to the son of so powerful a personage would have been very dangerous. To say she did not want to marry a pagan would have been to denounce herself as a Christian — that is, to deliver herself and her parents to the beasts. So very cleverly she told the boy that he had come too late, that she already loved another, and that she had sworn not to marry anyone else. Very disappointed, the governor's son went away.

But soon he came back to try again. He boasted to Agnes of all the riches he would give her if she agreed to become his wife — palaces, immense lands, thousands of slaves, jewels, treasures. But she answered, smiling, "He whom I love is still richer! He possesses the whole world; He has as many servants as He wishes; His palaces will soon rise in all the cities of the earth; and the treasures, the jewels He gives me are so rare that none can steal them." And the youth was even more astonished.

But he was still determined to marry Agnes. One day, he found himself alone with her in a deserted garden, and his disappointment turning to rage, he laid violent hands on her. But the angel appointed as her special protector intervened, and the youth fell to the ground — dead. Agnes was moved to pity at the sight; as a good Christian, she bore him no malice. She prayed fervently to Christ, and the young man rose to his feet.

It was an act of pity, of charity, but alas, the gentle maid received no thanks for it. Soon the rumor spread that it was in Christ's name that Agnes had restored her aggressor to life. And the governor gave orders for her arrest.

∞

When they came for her at her father's house, Agnes was praying. And at the very moment the guards were knocking at the door, she seemed to see the gates of Paradise opening wide to welcome her. Her courage increased tenfold in consequence. Without making the slightest attempt at resistance, she followed the officers before the judge whose special business it was to deal with Christians.

"Why is she not in chains, according to the law?" he demanded angrily.

"It was not necessary," answered the centurion in command of the guards. "She came without a word — and anyway, she is so young."

"The law is the law," insisted the judge. "Put handcuffs on her. I can see she is just as wily and obstinate as all the other Christians!"

A soldier fastened handcuffs around the girl's wrists. But she only smiled, shook her hands, and the irons fell off. Was there any need for an inquiry? Did not all this prove that she was a witch, one of those dangerous Christians who were believed to cast spells and to have the power to kill and to restore life as they pleased? Well, since her name meant "the most pure," they would soon see.

And the judge ordered Agnes to be thrown into a horrible tavern, a kind of ill-famed saloon frequented by slaves, soldiers, and gladiators, where drunken men spoke only of vile things and all took pleasure in evil living. But just as she was setting foot in this frightful place, what did they see at her side? A lion! A terrible lion that accompanied her like a big dog, its head against the girl's hands, but snarling and showing its fangs as soon as any man seemed to be coming near her. So a great circle formed around Agnes, at a safe distance, and she, in the midst, could continue to pray and to sing to the glory of God.

The judge's anger grew more violent. Would they never get the better of this witch? He had an enormous pile of fagots built up in one of the squares of Rome and summoned a crowd to witness the fine spectacle: the little Christian girl to be burned alive!

Hundreds of idlers hurried to the spot, many of them crowded together at the windows of neighboring houses. The executioners set fire to the pile. But . . . another miracle! Instead of devouring the martyr, the flames fell back fiercely to the right and left, as though by the force of a sudden strong wind. They reached the front rows of the onlookers, singeing their clothes and causing them to flee in panic. Motionless and calm in the midst of the confusion, Agnes recited her Hail Marys.

This business simply had to be stopped! And the judge ordered that she be beheaded. Of course, it would have been easy enough for the little saint to ask Christ for another miracle, and the executioner's sword would have fallen from his hands, or the executioner would have died of shock. But she had only one desire now — to find her beloved in Heaven, Jesus, her only spouse.

Without the least sign of agitation, she walked to the place of execution. She knelt down, lifted her eyes to Heaven and said a last prayer aloud, then bowed her head and with her own hands lifted the long tresses from her neck, so that they fell to the ground before her. Then she offered her neck to the executioner. "Do your duty, executioner!"

"You are too slow!" cried the judge, furious at Agnes's composure, and her gentle voice was heard repeating, "Yes, executioner, do your duty, you are too slow!" A few seconds later, the maiden's white dress was spattered dark red, and a new martyr joined the glorious band.

∞

This wonderful story had many wonderful sequels. Here are some of them.

Agnes had had a friend named Emerantina whom she loved dearly but had not succeeded in persuading to be baptized. Emerantina was a catechumen — that is, she was studying the Christian religion, but she had not yet decided to ask for baptism. On learning of her friend's death, Emerantina rushed to the cemetery on a day when many people were there. She cried out that she, too, was a Christian and started to reproach the pagans for committing such revolting crimes as to torture a child. The infuriated crowd seized her, threw her to the ground and stoned her to death. Yet another martyr had been born to Heaven!

There we see the power of example. A Christian author of the time wrote, "The blood of the martyrs was the seed of the Church . . ." By dying with such tranquil heroism, the martyrs heightened the faith, the courage, the desire for sacrifice of their brethren. They proved to the pagans that no power on earth could break their purpose. Their blood was like the seed which, falling into the earth, brings forth a tenfold harvest. The number of Christians increased in direct ratio to the violence of the Roman persecutions, and soon there were so many of them that it was no longer possible to kill them all.

The faithful came to pray at the tombs of the martyrs, imploring them to intercede with Almighty God in their favor. One day, as Agnes's parents were kneeling at their child's grave, Heaven seemed to open and a magnificent band of maidens came toward them, clothed in garments so beautiful that nothing like them had ever been seen on earth. Among them was Agnes, smiling, and at her side a little lamb of marvelous whiteness — doubtless a symbol of Christ, the Lamb of God. And it is in memory of this vision that to this day, on the feast of St. Agnes, the Pope blesses two perfectly white lambs, which are then led to a convent where the nuns spin and weave the wool to make the pallium, the special stole worn by archbishops.

On another occasion, a young princess named Constance, who was afflicted with the terrible disease of leprosy, came to Agnes's tomb to beg her to obtain a cure. The little martyr appeared to her and said, "This illness is the punishment for your evil living. When you stop sinning, when you have become as pure as I was, you will be healed." Constance understood the lesson; she obeyed and changed her ways. Having become an excellent Christian, she ordered a church to be built in honor of St. Agnes at the very spot in Rome where there still stands a very old and very beautiful church of that name.

In the following century, one of the most learned churchmen of the time, St. Ambrose, Archbishop of Milan, desiring to teach his flock the beauty of the virtue of purity, lovingly set down the marvelous story of St. Agnes, the little Christian martyr. It is his account that I have used to tell you the story in my turn.

∞

Blandina, the Slave Girl

This story takes us back to the year 177, and to the great city of Lyons in France. Lyons in those days was the capital of Gaul, the most populated of its cities and a great trading center for all the merchants of the Roman Empire. It contained many splendid houses, palaces, temples, and theaters whose ruins have now been uncovered. It was also a kind of religious capital to which the pagans from all parts of Gaul sent delegates for the celebration of the great festivals in honor of their gods. These ceremonies, dedicated to "Rome and Augustus," were also the occasion of trade fairs, of theatrical performances and circus shows, of a lot of drinking and plenty of gossip. Among such crowds, there could have been no lack of topics of conversation. And, of course, there was much talk about the Christians.

There was already a large number of Christians in Lyons. The reason was not far to seek. The merchants who were constantly arriving from Asia Minor, Egypt, or Greece had heard the gospel story. Many of them were already baptized, and they repeated the Good News and taught the doctrine of Jesus to those about them. Christianity thus came to France from the East. In Provence, for instance, the legend goes that Lazarus, whom Jesus raised from the dead, accompanied by his sisters, Martha and Mary, brought the gospel to the Marseilles region. And in Paris, they say that the first bishop of that city, the martyr St. Denis, was a Greek, a disciple of the great apostle Paul — as were also, apparently, the first bishops of other cities of France. In any event, the good seed sown by the men from the East put down magnificent roots in Gallic soil in this latter part of the second century, and there was probably no town without its community of the faithful. And that is precisely what annoyed the pagans.

∞

"The Christians to the lions!" "To death with the Christians!" "To the circus, all of them!" "Arrest them!" "Kill them!"

The cry spread like wildfire through the crowd gathered for the annual festivities. It would be entertaining to see Christians being burned alive, or to watch wild beasts tearing and devouring the quivering flesh of human beings!

"The Christians to the lions!" "The Christians to the beasts!"

The Roman governor who ruled Gaul in the emperor's name heard the cries of the infuriated mob. Had he been free, he might perhaps have taken no action against the Christians, since he knew they were innocent of any crime. But it would not be wise to disregard the passions of the people; he might be denounced to the emperor as a weakling and an accomplice of the Christian sect.

The most absurd rumors circulated in the crowd. The Christians, it was said, gathered at night to celebrate abominable ceremonies: they took a young child, covered him with flour, pierced him with daggers, and devoured his flesh. Such absurd tales were believed, and owing to them, the pagan priests were able to work up the people and incite them to fearful violence against the Christians.

Finally, in his palace, the governor realized that he could not avoid action. If he failed to satisfy the people, an uprising might take place for which the emperor would blame him most severely. Would it not be better to sacrifice a few dozen Christians? The Christians were of no great consequence, really. And so the order went out for their arrest.

They were seized at haphazard. Rich and poor, nobles and beggars, old and young, women and children. In the Church of Christ, there are only brethren; there is neither slave nor free, but all are equal in the divine love of the Master, all are equal in the face of death.

And that is how it came about that the most moving figure in this persecution at Lyons was a little slave girl not more than fifteen years old: Blandina, whose courage drew tears from the pagans themselves.

The Christians were arrested in the broad light of day, in the midst of great popular clamor. Soldiers marched into the houses of persons known to have been baptized. When they came out with their haul, the crowd insulted the prisoners, struck them, covered them with spittle; then they turned and ransacked and robbed their houses.

The Christians were led to the forum, the public square where the judges were to conduct the trial. What a mockery the trial was! Could all those threats and blows be called a cross-examination? As for the accused, they firmly confessed their faith, loudly claiming the name of Christians. The torturers were there, with their instruments all ready.

It was all so shameful, so thoroughly contrary to the law, that one of the spectators could no longer contain his indignation and rose to address the judges and the people. He was Vettius, a man of rank and one greatly respected in Lyons.

"The law," he declared, "allows any citizen to take the defense of an accused person. I shall therefore defend these men, these women, and these children. And I tell you, I, Vettius, a citizen of Lyons, that they have committed none of the crimes you charge them with, and that your so-called trial is an outrage . . ."

He could get no further; the judge interrupted him: "You are a Christian yourself, are you not?"

And in a ringing voice, Vettius replied, "Yes, I am!"

Immediately he, too, was seized and herded into the ranks of the accused.

Then the tortures began. They were indescribable. The mildest was to be bound to a rack while the torturers tore at one's body with iron hooks. Or to endure the frightful burning of red-hot iron plates thrust into one's flesh. A young priest named Sanctus endured such tortures for hours on end, but by a miracle of God, he could still move his limbs, his flesh remained whole, and his courage did not waver.

The ninety-year-old bishop of Lyons, Pothinus, was also brought before the judge. "Who is the god the Christians serve?" the judge asked him sarcastically.

"You will know Him when you are worthy to know Him," the saint replied.

Whereupon the soldiers fell upon the aged man, assailing him with their fists, kicking him, hurling at him whatever objects were in reach. Finally he was picked up, disfigured, bleeding, so exhausted that he could no longer stand, and he died in prison two days later.

The scenes of horror continued for many days. And they took place before the very eyes of the other Christians who were awaiting their turn, and who could thus see what they were going to suffer themselves. Is it astonishing that some of them should have been frightened and fallen away, agreeing to sacrifice to the heathen gods in order to escape such tortures? What is astonishing is that their number should have been so small — a dozen, perhaps — few enough beside so many heroes.

One of the last Christians to be brought to "trial" was a young slave girl named Blandina. Now, under the Romans, slaves were regarded as the lowest of the low. Indeed, they were not thought of as human beings at all but as objects that could be destroyed at will. But little Blandina was to prove that a fifteen-year-old slave girl could stand up to all the magistrates, soldiers, and torturers who tormented her.

They threatened her, assailed her with blows, but she remained unmoved.

"Confess what you have seen in your master's house. Tell us what ceremonies the Christians hold at night. Isn't it true that they kill young children and eat their flesh?"

Blandina answered calmly, "No, we do no harm. All we do is to love one another, to live fraternally, to be just, pure, charitable. Is that our crime?"

For hours they tortured her, and for hours she repeated the same words. And she was so firm and so brave that a woman in the crowd burst into tears and ran to the judge's stand. She was one of the Christians who had weakened and consented to deny Christ. Blandina's sublime courage had shattered her to the bottom of her soul, and she cried out, "Blandina is right! It isn't true that Christians commit the crimes you accuse them of! Eaters of human flesh, indeed! The only eaters of human flesh are yourselves, who feed on the frightful spectacle of their sufferings, who burn women and children alive or tear them apart!"

At once she was arrested all over again and thrown among those who were to die.

∞

Then the executions began. The immense amphitheater was filled with spectators. It is hard to imagine: thousands of people — perhaps not even bad people — coming to amuse themselves at the sight of the suffering and death of innocent persons!

One of the Christians, Attalus, was bound to a burning-hot iron chair and left to roast there like a piece of meat. He cried out to the crowd: "You see now that the eaters of human flesh are yourselves!" Another, Alexander, who had not been arrested with his brethren, came to the arena to encourage them; he spoke so well that the judge realized that he, too, was a Christian, ordered his arrest, and had his throat cut.

Now came the high point of the entertainment: the beasts were let out. They were of all kinds, all ravening, having deliberately been kept without food for a week. The lions sprang and roared; the leopards whined like furious cats; the bears, growling, padded up to the Christians as they stood chained together in groups of three or four and tore them apart limb from limb.

Blandina had been condemned to be thrown to the beasts. She was bound to a stake in the center of the arena, and to her fellow sufferers she seemed like a living image of Jesus crucified, of the Lord who was guiding them now and waiting for them in Heaven. Her masters and her friends, seeing how tiny and frail she was, had wondered whether she would have the strength to hold out to the end, or whether she would deny her faith. Little did they know that fiery soul!

The first day, she watched all the torments of her brethren without flinching. On her stake, she prayed and sang hymns; from time to time, she would call upon one or other of the martyrs to encourage him to die for Christ. None of the wild beasts would touch her, and she had to be returned to the jail. This happened several times; were the beasts sated? Or was this frail little creature too meager a morsel? Whatever the reason, Blandina was still alive.

As the week of executions drew to a close, she was brought back once again. This could not be allowed to go on! As for Blandina, she was as composed as ever, as full of faith and hope as always. Her only concern was about her friend Ponticus, a boy of the same age as herself; she was afraid he might not have the strength to die a martyr's death.

These were the only ones left now — two children. They had been scourged "to death," but they had survived. They had been "roasted," but they had not renounced their faith. The wild beasts had been released on them again, but the sated animals had simply sniffed and circled around them without touching them. Finally the butchers fell upon young Ponticus and slaughtered him. Blandina praised the Lord: her friend had died a saint!

She was quite alone now in the huge arena. The crowd, impressed finally by her heroism, called to her, "Abjure! Sacrifice to our gods! Your life will be spared!" And many said to one another, "Never has any woman been known to suffer as bravely as this slave girl!"

But she did not even answer. Her eyes were raised to Heaven, where she saw the Master waiting for her, beckoning to her. Finally her tormentors invented a new form of execution: they placed Blandina inside a great net, then let loose upon her a raging bull. The beast scooped her up with its horns and tossed her several times; the martyr's body fell to the ground with a noise of shattered bones. But she was still breathing, still murmuring prayers. Finally they slew her with a sword.

Thus died Blandina, patroness of all servant-maids, model for all children. Had she not proved for all the world to see that a person may be nothing in the sight of men yet very great in the sight of God?

∞

When all the Christians were dead, their poor remains were gathered up and exposed for a week so that the people could insult them further. "They must be burned," the heathen said, "because those pigheaded Christians insist that they can rise again. Their miserable remains must be scattered to the winds." So they burned them, swept up the ashes and threw them into the river Rhone. As though God, who can do all things, was not able to bring His witnesses back to life, those sublime men and women and children who for His sake had endured torture and death!

The martyrs of Lyons will rise again on the last day, with all the rest. They will be in the front ranks of the blessed band of the elect who sing an eternal *alleluia.* And among them will be a little slave girl, her face shining with glory — Blandina, in her final triumph over her tormentors!

Two Captives in Ethiopia

We move now to Tyre, around the year AD 335. This great Phoenician port had been famous for thousands of years for the trading expeditions it sent out to all points of the compass — as far north as the Hebrides, as far south as the shores of mysterious Africa. It was not merely an enormous warehouse filled with the most precious merchandise of the entire world; it was also an intellectual center where the best teachers were to be found, where the libraries were stacked with thousands upon thousands of books, where countless students gathered from far and near.

On this particular evening, a man was talking to two boys on a terrace overlooking the sea, and as he spoke, he watched the red sun setting behind the dark-green waters of the Mediterranean. His name was Metrodorus, one of the best-known professors of the city, an eminent philosopher, a geographer, too, and an excellent Christian. The older of the boys, Frumentius, was about fifteen, but his bearing, his serious air, and the attention with which he listened to his master's words made him appear more. The second boy, Aedesius, was only twelve, but he was alert and eager to learn.

What was their teacher telling them? "Do you remember," he asked them, "what happened just over twenty years ago? Our great emperor, Constantine, who reigns gloriously today in the city that bears his name — Constantinople — was at war at the time with his rival, Maxentius. He had already decided, in his inmost heart, to be baptized. And what happened just as he was about to fight the decisive battle on the banks of the Tiber?"

"I know," cried Frumentius. "He saw a shining cross appear in the sky, and he heard a voice saying, 'By this sign thou shalt conquer!' "

"Well said, my boy! And that is how Constantine, after his victory, became the protector of Holy Church. Since then, the nightmare of the persecutions has ended. It is no longer dangerous to declare one's faith in Christ. But do you think our task, as Christians, has also ended? Answer me!"

He motioned to the boys to return to the room where they studied. On the wall was a map of the Roman empire and all the surrounding countries.

"The places marked in red," said Metrodorus, "are those where our Lord's gospel has been taught."

"There aren't many, compared with the rest," said Aedesius.

"No, there are not enough. And do you remember what Christ commanded His disciples, the holy Apostles, before He returned to the Father?"

" 'Go, teach all nations' " answered Frumentius.

"Yes, Frumentius. 'Go, teach all nations.' That is the great law. That is the Master's command. It is not enough to give lessons to willing pupils, or to write books. We are called to another task, we who are witnesses of Christ crucified: to go to the countries where His name is not yet known, to which His message has not yet come."

They stepped out again upon the terrace, and while the moonlight turned the dark waters blue and transformed the sky into an immense pearly shell, Metrodorus went on talking to the boys. He told them the marvelous stories of the Apostles, how they had set off in all directions, even to the most dangerous lands, in obedience to our Lord's command. He told them that while Sts. Peter and Paul were being martyred in Rome, St. Andrew was pushing forward into the immense regions of Scythia (modern Russia); St. Mark was landing in Egypt; St. Thomas was approaching distant India; and St. Matthew was penetrating into the heart of Africa — mysterious Ethiopia. Thus, the good seed of the gospel had been sown in many lands, but an immense task still remained to be done. New apostles must return to those lands, help whatever groups of baptized persons existed there, win new souls for Christ. What a splendid adventure to set out for unknown lands, to discover new countries, new peoples, all for Christ and His holy religion!

It was very late, and the moon was already very high in the heavens when Metrodorus disclosed his great plan to his young friends.

∞

A few months later, two young boys were among the passengers on the Phoenician boat that put in at the port of Adulis, on the east coast of Africa. Metrodorus had a brother in those parts who was a merchant, and this brother was to help them carry out their designs. What designs? Nothing less than to carry the gospel to Ethiopia (we call it Abyssinia today), where St. Matthew was said to have taught and died a martyr, but where no Christians were left.

What was known about the land was not reassuring. Tremendous volcanoes spouting flames and lava; terrifying sheer-sided gorges dividing the mountains into separate "tables"; valleys so narrow and marshy as to be practically impassable. And rains . . .

what rains! Torrents, downpours lasting for months at a time, penetrating the sun-warmed tropical soil and causing great virgin forests to grow, with monstrous trees. Worse still, the beasts — panthers, lions, elephants, snakes. As for the people? Little was known about them with certainty. Add to that all the terrifying ideas the imagination could conjure up, and you will see that it really needed courage to set out on such an expedition.

But after some weeks' preparation, the caravan started out: a whole train of camels with their drivers, mules, packhorses, some forty men, and our two boys, amazed and thrilled at all they saw. As they approached the high country, the strange outlines of square-faced, table-topped mountains emerged against the horizon. The caravan moved slowly, constantly hindered by the tangled branches of trees lying across the track, or by the swift waters of a swollen river. Finally they reached the plateau. The air was fresh, there was less rain, and there stretched before their eyes an immense plain studded with great clumps of trees. And then —

Yells! A rain of arrows! Galloping horsemen! The woods must be filled with them. Roving bandits scouring the plain in search of loot had sighted the caravan from afar. Probably they thought this was one of those rich trading expeditions where all the camels were laden with precious goods. They were mistaken, but before they could realize their error, Metrodorus and the rest were falling under the assault.

The mules reared; the terrified camels threw off their drivers and fled at a great pace. In less than ten minutes, the frightful slaughter was completed. Of the forty brave men who had hoped to bring the good news of Christ to the kingdom of Ethiopia, there remained only dead or dying whom the bandits finished off with knives.

Nevertheless, it was in the Lord's design that Ethiopia should become Christian. And the instrument of that design was to be not the good Metrodorus, but his two pupils, Frumentius and Aedesius, whom he had prepared for that very task.

∞

When the first arrows came whistling through the air, accompanied by savage yells, Frumentius, who always had his wits about him, seized his younger friend's arm and shouted, "Let's jump!" They slid down from their high perch on the camel's back, picked themselves up, and raced to a nearby clump of trees, where they hid. From that spot they witnessed the whole horrible scene, terror-stricken. They saw their good master dying on the ground, his breast pierced, and could not even run out to give him their last embrace. They were sure this was their last hour, too.

Frumentius, squeezing his friend's hand, said to him, "Let's pray to the Lord to save us. Our only hope is in Him."

Soon one of the robbers spotted them and began walking in their direction, his spear dripping with blood. But before he could reach them, they heard someone shouting harsh-sounding words in a language they could not make out, and the man stopped dead in his tracks.

Another man — the leader, presumably — came up, pulled them out of their hiding place, and looked them over carefully. Clearly he was surprised to find children there. He had just realized that the caravan was not carrying rich merchandise or anything of value, and he was thoroughly perplexed. What could it all mean?

The leader called out an order, and the next moment, Frumentius and Aedesius were hoisted on a camel's back and bound to the saddle, one on either side, so tightly that they could not make a single movement. Then the camel got up off its knees and moved off at a trot.

∞

At last the painful journey was over. The boys were unshackled, but were so stiff and bruised that at first they could not stand. When they were finally able to get to their feet and look about them, they found themselves in the courtyard of a strange, red palace, with massive towers and walls bristling with beams standing straight up on end. After a little while, a lady came toward them, accompanied by two boys of about their own ages, and escorted by a whole train of elegantly dressed persons, of guards, and of servants carrying great plumed fans.

Frumentius and Aedesius gathered that they were in the presence of the queen and waited, holding their heads high, sure that they were about to receive their death warrant.

But to their great surprise, the lady spoke to them kindly, in their own tongue — Greek — although with a strong accent. Her skin was dark, the cast of her features agreeable. The two boys at her sides kept staring curiously at Frumentius and Aedesius, but they did not seem to wish them any harm. Astonished but very happy, our two young travelers realized that they were saved.

That was how Frumentius and Aedesius became what might be described as pages at the court of the King of Ethiopia, or the Negus, as he was called. They were captives, but no one tried to check their movements or prevent them from leaving. In any case, they could never have escaped, being so far from their own country, and having no means at all of getting through the dangerous forest. The queen protected them.

As a little girl, she had been sent by her parents to the great Egyptian city of Alexandria to learn Greek and something of Greek and Egyptian civilization. So she questioned the boys at length, asking them about their studies, and she was very impressed by their intelligence. Frumentius, especially, was very advanced and could have held his own with many of his elders in such subjects as history, geography, arithmetic, astronomy, and music. The queen enjoyed talking with him, for there was no one else in her great red palace who could have spoken to her of all these things.

It was decided, therefore, that Frumentius and Aedesius should teach Dajan and Bako — the two sons of the king and queen — their own language and whatever they had learned themselves. They were to live with the princes, take their meals with them, play with them. The young captives were fortunate indeed!

But although they were well satisfied with their lot, they did not forget why their teacher had brought them to this land, or why he had died. It was in order to serve Christ that they had left Tyre with Metrodorus. Since he was no longer with them, and they alone survived of the bearers of the gospel, it was for them to teach the message of salvation.

They went about it without hesitation. At that time, the Ethiopians still worshiped idols, animals they believed sacred, something like the golden calf of the Bible or the Apis bull of ancient Egypt. The two young apostles began to show their companions how ridiculous that was, how calves and bulls could not be gods, and how the true God was one, invisible, all-powerful. Then they told them all they knew about Jesus, about the wonderful message He had brought the world, about His death on the Cross to redeem mankind, about His Resurrection and His glory.

Sometimes the queen herself came to listen to them, and since she had already met Christians during her stay at Alexandria, she reflected the more deeply on the matter. Soon a little group formed around the two Christian boys — young people who knew the gospel message and loved Christ. Of course, the heathen priests were very angry, but what could they do? The queen's protection prevented them from seizing the two young captives and putting them to death, as they would certainly have liked to do.

Months passed. The king, who had long been ill, died, and his elder son, Dajan, came to the throne in his place. The evening of his coronation, the young king called Frumentius and said to him, "I am king now, and all-powerful. You, my friend, have taught me to love Christ, to know the most splendid of all teachings, and I want all my people to know them, too. A caravan is outside the palace waiting for you, well equipped with guards and arms. You will leave with Aedesius, return to the Christians, and tell their leaders what I desire. Let them send me learned priests and very holy monks, and let the gospel be preached throughout my land!"

∞

A few months later, the great Patriarch of Alexandria, St. Athanasius, was at work in his study — and goodness knows he had enough to do, what with fighting heresies and writing magnificent works on the Scriptures and on the lives of the early saints — when he was told that two boys, strangely attired, were asking to speak to him. He might perhaps have refused to see them because he did not want to be interrupted in his work, but the voice of the Lord, which speaks silently in the hearts of saints, made it plain to him that he must receive them.

Frumentius told the whole story to the wise archbishop. He told him that over there, in far-off Ethiopia, was a king who desired baptism for himself and his people. Athanasius listened attentively and asked many questions. The boy was clearly inspired by God!

"Yes," he told him, "I shall send priests to your friends. Yes, they shall belong to Christ! But I want the leader of the mission to be you, child, whom Christ Himself has protected and marked out for His service. You will study as hard as you can, and when you know enough, I shall consecrate you bishop. Then, in the Lord's name and under my authority, you shall set out to govern the new church you have brought into being."

And that is how St. Frumentius, who had carried the gospel to Ethiopia, came to be chosen the first bishop of that land.

∞

Genevieve, the Shepherdess

One fine clear morning about fifteen hundred years ago, two grave men were walking on the Roman road leading from Paris to Rouen. From their blue linen mantles and blue tunics you could tell they were bishops, for blue in those days was the color set aside for the leaders of the Christian Church.

One of them was tall and thin, and gnarled as an ancient tree; his name was Lupus, and he was Bishop of Troyes, in Champagne. The other was smaller and suppler; this was the Bishop of Auxerre, Germanus. They had left Paris before daybreak, wishing to reach the little town of Argenteuil by noon to venerate the precious relic of the first Bishop of Paris, the glorious martyr St. Denis.

They had recited their prayers before the three great crosses set on the sharp rise of ground known as Mont Valerian. Then they had gone on again, through the lovely meadows where flocks of sheep peacefully cropped the sweet grass. It was spring, a beautiful time of year in the Paris region, when the air is fresh and keen, when smiles come readily to people's lips, when birds trill merrily the whole day through.

But the loveliness of the morning did not seem to cheer our two prelates. What was troubling them so? As a matter of fact, for anyone the least bit observant, there were plenty of reasons for worry in that year AD 432. Western Europe was undergoing a terrible ordeal: some twenty-five years earlier, the great barbarian invasions had begun. The German tribes that the Roman legions had held in check for centuries on the Rhine and the Danube rivers had finally broken through and were pouring in huge successive waves into the finest provinces of the Roman empire: Visigoths, Ostrogoths, Vandals, Burgundians — the names differed and even the appearances, but all were invaders, all bent on conquest, all given to robbery and violence in one form or another, all settling in the best cities and taking over whatever they wanted for their own use. Look, there were some of them coming along the road right now — Alani, probably — tall, blond, blue-eyed, speaking a harsh tongue. Alas for the empire, the glorious empire of Rome under the dominion of these barbarians!

But could one even speak of an empire at all? Rome, the pride of the world, was practically a dead city. At the new capital, Ravenna, the unworthy descendants of the great emperors were frittering away their days in wild living, intrigues, and palace revolutions. The Roman legions were commanded by Germans! And the two bishops agreed that these distressing events must have been willed by Providence. The haughty empire that had thought it could halt the advance of Christ's gospel, that had tortured and killed the saints of God, was now being punished for its crimes.

Nevertheless, all was not lost. One great force remained whole and unimpaired in the midst of the general ruin: the Church. Guided by their bishops — and particularly by the first of the bishops, the Pope — the faithful were trying to convert and civilize the barbarians. Thanks to the Christians, whose numbers were now considerable, a new world was emerging in which Germans and Romans would be reconciled, united through Baptism. So the fifth century, as you see, was an important one, and it is not surprising that St. Lupus and St. Germanus should have been talking about all these things, and that they should have looked grave.

As they went down an incline in the road — at but a short distance they could see the blue ribbon of the Seine winding through the meadows — a little girl of Nanterre who was guarding her sheep in a pasture recognized them by their clothes and knelt down, making a big Sign of the Cross. The bishops replied with gestures of blessing. Then they stopped.

What had happened? This was not the first time a shepherdess had knelt before them to receive their blessing. What was so special about this one? Quite possibly neither of them could have explained just then. But both were saints, and the Spirit of God speaks in the hearts of saints, showing them things that are hidden from ordinary men. The moment the little girl knelt down, something like a mysterious current flowed through them, and they seemed to hear a call. Was the sky purer and brighter above the child? Germanus, being the more agile of the two bishops, jumped the ditch bordering the road and walked up to the little shepherdess.

She was not more than twelve years old, tall for her age, but pale and thin — very thin in her long, gray wool tunic. Seeing the bishop approaching, she remained on her knees and bowed her head, then raised it and turned her great blue eyes upon him.

"What is your name?" asked Germanus.

"Genevieve," the little girl replied.

"And your father's?"

"Severus."

"He's a Roman?" the bishop asked.

"Yes, but my mother is Greek."

"Is this your parents' flock?"

"Yes, and over there, my lord Bishop, you can see our house and our fields."

"You are a good Christian?"

"I try to be."

Why should these very simple words have moved the men of God so deeply? It seemed to them as though an angel of the Lord were speaking through the lips of this child who was so unassuming and so good.

"Ah, Genevieve," cried Germanus, "I know it now! The Lord has led us to you. For as soon as I saw you, His voice sounded in my heart and I knew that He had willed your birth, that choirs of angels sang at your cradle and that you would have a very important task to fulfill on earth for God and for the Church. Rejoice, my little child, for He will do great things through you — He whose name is holy!"

And little Genevieve, not in the least afraid, but filled with deepest joy, replied, like Mary to the angel: "Behold the handmaid of the Lord. May it be done unto me according to thy word."

❈

Imagine how astonished the good folk of Nanterre must have been when they saw little Genevieve, the shepherdess, Severus's and Geroncia's daughter, coming through the fortified gate of the town escorted by two bishops. And what bishops! There was no Christian in the region who had not heard of Bishop Germanus of Auxerre and Bishop Lupus of Troyes.

As soon as they recognized the pale blue tunics and mantles, the idlers strolling near the ramparts ran to alert their friends and relatives. Soon huge crowds had formed in the streets. And the people of Nanterre all wondered what it meant, and why the two prelates were accompanying Genevieve, one on her right, the other on her left, each holding one of her hands.

The three were heading for the church. All the clergy were gathered on the steps of the church, as astonished as everyone else. The little altar boy who carried the golden cross almost let it drop upon seeing his friend Genevieve in such company. The two bishops walked straight up the nave toward the altar, where they knelt down, and Genevieve did the same. Then, together, they began the hymn of thanksgiving, the *Te Deum*, which Christians love to sing when they want to thank God for His goodness; and all the people who had crowded into the church after them made the responses, verse by verse.

At the end, the Bishop of Auxerre turned around to face the people and raised his hand:

"Christians of Nanterre, I have great news for you!" he said. "This little girl of yours, this little Genevieve, was born for the glory of God, that she might do great things in His service. I tell you this in very truth, for the Holy Spirit revealed it to me when I saw this child guarding her sheep in the meadow. And I prophesy further that when she is older, she will guard not sheep but men, and not in the valley of the Seine alone but throughout the land of Gaul. Alleluia! Great is the Lord!"

Then he bent down to address the little girl who was still kneeling at the foot of the altar:

"Genevieve, do you wish to consecrate yourself to Christ for your whole life and live as His spouse, in purity, in humility, and in charity?"

And again Genevieve repeated, "Behold the handmaid of the Lord. May it be done unto me according to thy word!"

It was all just a little too beautiful, and as usual, the Devil had to put his oar in to thwart God's designs. Genevieve's father, Severus, was a Christian through and through, upright, hardworking, and generous, and Bishop Germanus's words had filled him with joy. But her mother, Geroncia, was a foolish, frivolous, vain woman, concerned only with fine clothes and pleasures.

When she learned what had happened, the Devil suggested a thousand complaints to her. If Genevieve went to live in a convent in Paris, as she had announced, who would guard the sheep, do the cooking, clean the house? For, as a matter of fact, the little girl did the work of a servant-maid, sparing her lazy mother the need to touch a dust-rag or a pot. They would have to find another maid . . . Severus was letting the headstrong girl lead him by the nose. The two bishops had had no business to meddle in what was no concern of theirs.

Since her nagging got her nowhere, she went further: she forbade Genevieve to go to church. Then, one day, when she saw her daughter slipping into the church to join two other girls who had also vowed to give themselves to God, she fell on her and began beating her with all her might. And then . . .

Suddenly Geroncia screamed with fright. No, this was not one of those cries of rage that had been on her lips a moment before. What had happened? She stretched out her arms, turned around and around, touched her eyes. She was blind! Blind in an instant! But do you think she understood the terrible lesson? Far from it. She tried to grab Genevieve to hit her again. "You wretch, you have cast a spell upon me! Witch! Sorceress!"

For days, Geroncia nursed her fury. Life was hard indeed at the farm: nothing but cries and complaints and reproaches the livelong day. But Genevieve bore her mother no malice. She simply prayed harder still, imploring Almighty God to make her mother understand her sin, to pardon her, and to heal her. And finally her fervent prayers were answered. One day, as she was drawing water from the well and pouring it from the pail into the pitcher, her mother came up to her, tapping the ground with a stick.

"Genevieve, make the Sign of the Cross over this water, and I will bathe my eyes in it."

"What are you asking me, Mother?" cried the terrified girl. "I cannot perform a miracle!"

"My child," answered Geroncia in a changed voice, "I have to tell you something. I realize how I have sinned, and I have asked pardon of the Lord."

A moment later, Geroncia was bathing her eyes in the water her daughter had blessed. Suddenly she uttered a cry of joy . . . And the next day she herself took Genevieve to the convent in Paris, behind the church of Notre-Dame, as Bishop Germanus of Auxerre had decided.

∞

That was how Genevieve, the shepherdess of Nanterre, became a nun and was able to devote her life — a long one — to the Lord. She was also able to fulfill Bishop Germanus's other prophecy: she did, in fact, become the spiritual shepherdess of the whole land of Gaul.

About fifteen years later, in 449, the news spread through Paris and the surrounding region that the Huns were on their way — those terrible Mongol horsemen, whose very name froze people's blood, whose leader, Attila, was so fierce that he had been named "the Scourge of God." Genevieve was about thirty at the time, and abbess of her monastery.

All the people of Paris revered her for her infinite charity, her endless generosity. Consequently, when they heard of the approaching peril, they rushed to her crying, "Save us, for we are about to perish!" An absurd move, it would seem; how should a weak woman, a religious, stand up to those beasts of prey? The men were practically desperate, and many talked of fleeing the city.

"Leave Paris," exclaimed Genevieve, "and take to the roads! Why, that would be courting massacre! For my part, I shall not leave. Let the men flee, if they will. I shall remain with my sisters and all the women who wish. And we shall pray so hard that God will end by hearing us." The men listened to the saint, and the miracle took place. Paris did not fall into the hands of the Mongol horsemen. The shepherdess had saved her flock.

From that time forward, everyone regarded Genevieve as the supernatural guide sent by God to the people of Gaul. King Clovis had no better counselor than the nun whose convent now stood on the hill known today as the Montagne Sainte-Genevieve. Since the king's palace was at the foot of the hill, the saint and the king could often be seen walking side by side in the royal gardens, discussing important affairs of state and Church. Clovis even asked that, when he died, he might be buried near the holy shepherdess.

And at the very end of her life, Genevieve again acted as God's shepherdess of her people. Torn by civil strife, Paris was in extreme want, to the point of being without bread. So Genevieve, worn out though she was with age, set out on the roads to beg for wheat for her poor Parisians. She went all the way to Champagne, to Beauce, to Normandy in her quest, and she returned by way of the river Marne with several boatloads of provisions. Once again the good shepherdess had rendered good service to those whom God committed to her care.

Since her death, St. Genevieve has remained the protectress of Paris. Prayers requesting her intercession are daily recited at church services in the capital city of France. The Montagne Sainte-Genevieve is a favorite place of prayer. There, in the old church of Saint-Etienne-du-Mont, her relics repose, enclosed in a magnificent casket of gold and enfolded in the love of generations of her countrymen.

St. Brendan and the Boy from the North

Outside the tempest howled. What a tempest! Winds roaring, waves like mountains hammering at the cliffs as though they would break them to pieces. The night seemed to be in the power of monstrous beasts ready to devour every human creature. It would go hard indeed with anyone afloat at such an hour.

In the monastery, the monks were at their prayers. Behind the enormous granite walls broken only by narrow window shafts, the tumult of the ocean was but a distant rumbling. Psalm followed psalm, each half of the choir chanting the verses in turn. The low, squat church was lit up only by the candles on the altar, with here and there an oil lamp at the end of the choir stalls casting its yellowish glow on the beams and joists of the roofing. The kneeling forms of the monks were barely visible in their brown homespun habits; only their tonsured heads showed palely in the gloom.

A door opened noiselessly, and a dark figure glided rapidly between the rows of chanting monks toward the stall of the abbot, who was distinguishable by the tall crozier at his side. Every night, while the community chanted the office, one or other of the brethren in turn remained at the watchtower, situated at a point of the monastery directly overlooking the sea. Shipwrecks were not uncommon on this Breton coast battered by fierce winds and waves. The monk on duty would scan the immense expanse of water and give the alarm if he spied a ship in distress.

On this particular night, the watchman hurried down from his tower, made his way to the choir, and after performing the customary prostrations before the Father Abbot, gave the distress signal — arms raised to heaven, then three genuflections. Whereupon St. Brendan struck the floor with his crozier, and immediately the chanting ceased. In the silence that followed, the booming of the ocean seemed to grow louder and more menacing.

"To save our brothers' lives is even more pleasing to God than to chant our prayers. Come, the Lord summons us to our duty!"

The next minute, they were all outside. Some of them, at the lookout, gazed out into the night, where the fitful glimmer of a pale moon lit up a boat that was tossing on the waves and keeling over. The others had already reached the little dock and were getting out the lifeboat that had often snatched the shipwrecked from the jaws of death. And once again, obedient only to the voice of their Christian conscience and at the risk of their own lives, St. Brendan's monks pulled out into the raging waters.

∞

"He's alive!" said Brother Cadoc, who was something of a doctor. And in fact, the slender form was moving a little, and a trace of color was returning to the livid face under its crown of blond hair plastered down by the salt water. A strange story! The rescuers had found only one survivor from the shipwrecked vessel, this little boy of ten or eleven tied to one of the galley benches to prevent him from being swept overboard. Where, then, was the crew? The body of one sailor had been found in a corner, killed probably by something falling. The others must have been swept away by the enormous waves breaking over the deck.

St. Brendan and the Boy from the North

"Yes, he's alive. God be praised!" answered Father Abbot, who had been bending over the child's breast. And in a loud voice he intoned a hymn of thanksgiving in which the others joined. At that moment, the little boy woke up and opened his eyes . . .

That is how the boy who would one day be known as Edwin of Iceland came to find a home on the coast of Brittany, thanks to the charity and the courage of St. Brendan's monks. For once they had warmed him up and fed him and put him in their best bed, they would not hear of letting him go. Had not God, in His holy providence, clearly shown that He wished the boy to live in the monastery? And anyway, all these rugged men felt a secret tenderness for this lovely child with his fresh pink cheeks and flaxen hair.

So it was decided that he should be brought up in the monastery, and that good Brother Gildas, the youngest and gentlest of the monks, should be especially detailed to look after him and instruct him. Later on, they would have one more brother in the monastery.

But the boy had a hard time of it at first. When the monks tried to ask him questions, it soon became clear that he knew neither Breton nor Latin. He spoke an incomprehensible tongue made up, it seemed, of words that went on and on forever and which none of the monks had ever heard before. At first he would always be found at the lookout post, or next to the watchman, his gray eyes desperately searching the horizon. What was he hoping to see? A strange shore? A boat on the open waters?

But after a time, a change came over him. He began speaking a few words of Breton; soon he was able to express himself quite easily. He even learned Latin, and his young voice could be heard among the deep voices of the monastic choir, rising light and clear like water bubbling from a spring. And often during recreation, when the rule allowed the monks to talk to one another, the boy from the sea would talk, too.

He insisted that far, far north, where the mists and storms came from, there were lands inhabited by other peoples. He would talk of the times he used to hunt and fish with his father and brothers aboard a light skiff propelled by a kind of double-bladed oar. He described the shoals of fish that one could see through the clear, green water, fish packed so tightly that they looked like a great block of stone. And he told also of extraordinary animals, some of them with gray fur skins and gentle eyes, others huge — "bigger than a boat," he insisted. The monks would laugh, thinking all this was childish exaggeration.

But St. Brendan listened to these strange stories and pondered deeply. Far, far away, then, there were lands inhabited by men. And those men, most certainly, knew nothing of the word of God! Was it not clear that by sending him this child, God was commanding His servant to preach the gospel in those lands, to baptize those men? And a plan began to take shape in St. Brendan's mind.

∞

You should know that at this period of history — the sixth century — the Christians were very active in western Europe. Many countries of Europe had not yet heard of Christ, but countless were the missionaries who hastened there to bring them the word of God. Whether it meant crossing the dark and dangerous and almost impenetrable forests of Germany, or venturing on the North Sea with its fierce storms, the messengers of Christ never hesitated to risk their lives so that the gospel might be preached.

We would never finish were we to try just to name those missionary heroes. All we shall say here is that the Bretons held a very high place among them. Whether they lived in the islands we now call Great Britain, or on the Breton peninsula of France, their dream was always to explore far-distant lands, to undertake daring missions — "peregrinations for Christ," as they called them. St. Patrick, two centuries earlier, had set the pattern when he boldly landed on the Irish shore and proceeded to evangelize the whole of that great island. And now there were men like St. Columbanus and his twelve companions, who had launched their magnificent missionary expedition into Gaul. And so many others . . .

St. Brendan dreamed of following such examples. Unknown islands, pagan souls to be baptized — the attraction was irresistible. For hours on end he could be seen walking beside little Edwin, the child from the sea, plying him with questions.

∞

Finally, one Sunday, after the high Mass in the monastery, Father Abbot assembled his monks in chapter and said to them something of this sort: "Our abbey is thriving now, and my work here is done. The Lord has shown me that a new duty calls me. I am therefore going to leave. I shall sail due north, to the land where — so the child God sent us assures me — there are souls waiting to be baptized."

Imagine the excitement among the monks! All wanted to join the great abbot in this venture upon the uncharted seas, in this most astonishing of "peregrinations for Christ." Eleven were chosen; with little Edwin as ship's boy, that made twelve. As Christ had had twelve Apostles, was it not fitting that St. Brendan should have twelve faithful followers at his side?

The best boat of the monastic fleet was carefully prepared for the voyage. It was stocked with provisions, with animal skins for protection against the cold, with sufficient arms. But the missionaries' principal equipment was plenty of faith and courage! They certainly needed those virtues to set out for those unknown lands where there lived so many terrifying beasts, where perhaps, so the tale went, the very gates of Hell lay open.

They put to sea. At first, all went smoothly, with no incident to relieve the monotony. The wind was behind them, filling their sails. Sometimes they passed through fog banks. Sometimes great flights of birds with huge wings would wheel over their boat. Then, gradually, the water of the sea changed. So far, it had been clear and restless; now it became still — almost stagnant, it seemed — very dark green, in the grip of an icy cold. Huge sheets of ice kept drifting past them. The monks almost killed themselves with rowing, both to make headway and to get warm; they wept with fatigue and their tears turned to ice on their cheeks. Did they have to go on?

"Yes! Yes!" little Edwin would cry. Since they had reached this cold, eerie region, he had not tried to hide his joy. He would cry out in his own tongue, a tongue he had not spoken for two years past. He recognized the seascape of his early childhood; these were the waters he had so often sailed with his father in search of fish. And all the things that worried the good monks were natural and familiar to the boy.

Plenty of astonishing incidents occurred. For instance, one night the watchman roused all the others with great shouts. On the sea, not far from the boat, there rose up a great, irregular-shaped mass, shining in the moonlight. It was not an island, for it was slowly drifting; at the same time, it had peaks and hollows like a small mountain. Was it a boat? No one had ever seen the like. As it drew closer, it seemed to become almost transparent, with blue lights and green shadows. Crowding together near the front of the boat, the thirteen gazed excitedly at the strange object.

St. Brendan and the Boy from the North

"Do you know this floating island, Edwin?" asked St. Brendan. "Have you ever seen any like it before?"

The boy explained. Yes, he had often seen islands like this when he was a very little boy. Still farther north, the land was covered with enormous glaciers reaching all the way down to the coast. Sometimes a giant fragment would split off and be swept away by the tides and currents, drifting at random in the ocean. That, of course, is how icebergs are formed; but St. Brendan and his companions had never heard of icebergs.

After hearing Edwin's explanation, Father Abbot decided that they would land on the floating island and celebrate Mass there. And so they did, setting up an altar in a huge cave of ice. As the sun had come out, and was shining through the blue and green ice masses of the walls, you would have thought they were in a great crystal cathedral with sparkling stained-glass windows. And St. Brendan, who celebrated the Mass, was clothed in a chasuble made, it seemed, of a marvelous rainbow!

Some days later, the lookout man announced another discovery. This time it was most definitely an island. A long island, not very high above the water line, oval-shaped, yellowish-gray in color. Good Brother Cadoc immediately suggested that they should do as they had with the crystal island — that is, celebrate Mass there. But Edwin, standing motionless in the front of the boat, was very carefully examining the island. It did seem strange — not a plant on it, not an animal, just a kind of crust that looked like half-dried mud.

Finally the little ship's boy went over to St. Brendan and respectfully kissed his ring. "Good Father," he said, "we should not land on what you think is an island. It is not land, but a fish!"

At this, all who heard him burst out laughing. A fish that size! Who had ever seen the like? And where was its head or its tail?

Some of the monks, the youngest, jumped into the landing boat and began rowing toward the yellowish island. Having landed, they called to the others, "See! It is a little island!"

Then they lit a fire and began preparing their dinner, all the while loudly singing a hymn of praise, so that the Lord might bless this land which they had won for Him. But then — the island began to shake and heave and roll like some huge balloon in a pond; then suddenly it got under way. It did not take the good brothers long to jump into the water and swim back to the boat, to the gibes and jeers of the rest. Soon the whale — you have guessed, of course, that it was a whale — had gathered speed, and all they could see of it was the double jet of water it sent up into the air, and the little red glow of the fire on its back.

I expect you would like to know how this strange expedition ended. Well, one day they finally sighted some real land. Extraordinary things were taking place at the time, seeming to portend grave events to come. For instance, the sun no longer set; it moved around the horizon without disappearing; at what should have been midnight, it was bright daylight. And in the blue-green light of those strange northern days that Edwin, so he said, knew well but could not explain, the island looked sinister, black and gray.

From time to time, they could see dark-red lights on the island, like the lights of a forge, and also immense jets that must have been boiling water, for they gave out tremendous clouds of steam. For all the monks' valor, the country they were heading for did not seem very welcoming. But Edwin was beside himself with joy, and kept calling out things in his own language, then running over to his dear Father Brendan and kissing his hands and saying, "My country! It's my country!"

But just as they were approaching land, the island began to make great rumbling noises. Then the rumblings turned into flames, and strange objects — stones, it seemed — shot up into the air. Then, to complete this disturbing picture, the monks saw creatures such as they had never seen before — like big gray dogs, but with almost human heads — jumping into the sea.

"They are devils!" cried one of the crew. "We've reached the gates of Hell! Woe to us! Lord, have mercy on our souls!"

But this time, too, Edwin was able to set their minds at rest. No, he told them laughingly, this was not Hell; this was his country, the great island we know today as Iceland. And those forms they took for demons were only seals. The noises, flames, and jets of stones came from volcanoes; there were a number of volcanoes on the island, and one got used to them, as they did not do much damage. Encouraged by their ship's boy, St. Brendan and his companions pushed on to the shore. Their dear young Edwin was the first to jump to land and to introduce the newcomers to the men who had come running down to the water's edge. And that is how Iceland first received the messengers of Christ.

Odilia, the Blind Princess

High on a ridge of the Vosges Mountains, overlooking the rich plain watered by the Rhine river, there stands a convent beloved of all the people of Alsace. The view is always beautiful, whether the sun is shining or the rain comes streaming down, whether the pine forests are wrapped in mist or the mountainsides are bathed in bluish light. Twenty towns, three hundred villages — that is what you can see from the marvelous convent terrace. And in the distance, the rose-colored spire of Strasbourg Cathedral pointing straight up into the sky. This hallowed spot, where prayers have risen unceasingly to God for twelve hundred years, is the convent of St. Odilia, made glorious by the patron saint of Alsace.

∞

We are back in the eighth century of our era — the century of Charles Martel ("the Hammer"), who halted the Arab advance at Poitiers; of his son, Pepin le Bref ("the Short"), who prevailed on the Pope to grant him the title of king; and of Pepin's son, Charles, whose courage and genius were later to earn him the name of Charlemagne ("Charles the Great").

Alsace, in those days, was ruled by Adalric, a prince famous both for his bravery and for his brutality. Nothing, so far, had ever gotten the better of him; there was no enemy he had not defeated, no bear pursued by his dogs he had not killed. And yet a great sorrow overshadowed his life: he and his wife had no children. And that meant that after his death, his beautiful Alsace would be pillaged and shared out among his greedy neighbors. The horrible prospect gave him no rest.

They grieved so much, both Adalric and Bereswindis, his wife, that they decided to retire from the world and live high up in the Vosges to meditate on their sorrow. They chose the steepest slope, protected on one side by a cliff and on the other by an impassable wall of rocks, and there they had their new castle built, the Hohenburg, or "high castle." Bereswindis, who was very pious and well read in the Scriptures, had a convent erected near her new residence where nuns were to pray with her that she might have a child.

And God heard her prayers. The duchess was able to inform her husband that soon he would have great joy. But alas, the joy was short-lived, for the little girl who was born to them, so pretty with her fair skin and blond hair, had one distressing defect: her eyes remained closed. She would be blind for life! When Duke Adalric heard this, he fell into a terrible rage. So God had granted his wish only to disappoint him even more! Better not to have had any child at all than this wretched little blind girl. Would not all his people be whispering that a curse rested on their ruler?

And so, when Bereswindis asked him what name the child should be given at baptism, he answered, "None! I forbid anyone to baptize this misbegotten creature who brings shame upon my name! Let her be killed instantly and her body thrown to the swine!"

The unhappy mother fell on her knees before him, pleading with him to let her little one live. But in vain. She suggested that

the child be taken far away and brought up in secret, without anyone ever being told who her parents were. But Adalric remained
unrelenting; this child brought shame upon him; let her be done
away with! So in the night, Bereswindis took the baby, wrapped
her up warmly, placed her in a little box, and stole out of the castle. She made her way to the nearby river Ehn and placed the frag-
ile craft upon the waters. Then she returned to her room and fell
to prayer. God, who could do everything, had saved little Moses
drifting on the Nile; would He not have pity on this innocent
creature, too?

That same night, the miller of Obernai awoke with a start. The
familiar sound of the mill wheel turning and the water splashing
had suddenly ceased. The miller got out of bed to see what had
happened. Something was blocking the machinery. On looking
closer, he found that it was a large box covered with a lid. He
opened it. Inside was a little girl, very much alive, whimpering
quietly, her eyelids closed. Bereswindis's little girl was saved.

The first years of her life were spent at the mill of Obernai. The
miller's wife took her in and cared for her most lovingly, and the
fact that the child was blind only added to her pity. No one came
to claim the abandoned mite, and her good foster-mother's one
idea was to keep her for good. But the neighbors were talking.
Where had the child come from? Did she not have any parents?
There was something very queer about this story of a baby floating
down the river. Maybe, people began to whisper, maybe the child
had been stolen?

To put a stop to this ugly gossip, the miller's wife decided to
place the little girl in the care of the good Sisters who lived up
there on the mountainside, near the castle. They were said to be so
gentle, so loving. So she brought them the child, and that is how
Bereswindis's daughter came to live in the convent built by her

own mother, right next to her father's castle. Alas, the duchess was dead, consumed with grief at the loss of her only child.

The nuns who brought her up were more and more amazed, with every year that passed, at the child's sweetness, obedience, piety, and intelligence. Her eyes remained closed, but it seemed that in the darkness she could see things hidden from others. When she was five or six years old, she spoke like a grown-up — better, even, than many grown-ups. When she prayed, all the radiance of Heaven seemed to be reflected in her gentle features. "A little saint," the good nuns murmured to each other. "We have a little saint in our midst!"

Far away beyond the Rhine, there lived a bishop named Erard who also had a great name for holiness. One night, as he was praying fervently according to his habit, Christ Himself appeared to him, saying, "Go into the Vosges mountains to the place I shall show you. There you will find a convent in which a little blind girl lives. No one knows her name or her parentage. She has never been baptized. You are to baptize her, and as soon as the holy water is poured over her, her eyes will open to the light."

Erard obeyed instantly. He set out, crossing Bavaria, Thuringia, the Black Forest, the Rhine. A mysterious power guided his steps, and he never lost his way. Finally he arrived at the convent, where the nuns received him with great reverence. They were astonished indeed when he asked to see the little blind girl who lived among them. And their astonishment was even greater when they heard her cry, after the bishop had baptized her, "I can see!" The whole community fell to their knees to thank God for the miracle.

The name Bishop Erard gave the little girl at baptism — Odilia — had been told him by Christ Himself. It is a lovely name borne to this day by many girls of Alsace, and of other regions.

Odilia, of course, stayed on at the convent, and the older she grew, the more exceptional were her virtues. What she loved most were the long, beautiful services at which the whole community sang to the glory of God. As for herself, she ate only barley bread and boiled vegetables, and slept on a bearskin on the floor. But while she was hard on herself, she was marvelously good to others, especially to the poor, the helpless, and the sick, for whom she begged the Mother Abbess to build a hospital.

The fame of her holiness began to spread. All over Alsace, right down to the smallest hamlet, people were talking of the miracles connected with Odilia.

There was the convent well, for instance: since Odilia's baptism, when she had received her sight, the well had been filled to the brim with water that healed all ailments of the eyes.

Or the altar cruets, which the Sister sacristan had forgotten to fill for Mass: just as the priest noticed they were empty, Odilia said a prayer, and at once they were filled with wine and water.

Or the lime trees that had suddenly grown to give her shade . . . That was on a very hot August day as she was coming back from visiting the poor in a neighboring town. She was looking vainly for a little shade in the sun-baked plain when an angel came down from Heaven and planted three lime branches in the earth. In a matter of seconds, three full-grown lime trees were standing there.

Thus, Odilia reached her fifteenth year — beautiful, good and pure and always pleasing to God.

∞

In the whole land, there was only one who would hear nothing of the whole story — Adalric, the terrible duke. On every side, people kept telling him that the little saint in the convent was his own daughter, the blind child he had wanted to have killed. They advised him to take her back to his castle and acknowledge her as his daughter. But each time, he burst into a rage again, threatening to strike those who spoke to him like that.

One morning, as he was coming home from the hunt along a forest path, his horse suddenly stopped. At the foot of a tree there sat a poorly dressed woman — a nun — a heavy sack at her side. She seemed very tired.

"You there, girl! What's the matter?" Adalric called from his saddle.

The nun raised her head, and immediately the duke's blood seemed to run cold. That lovely young face — the image of his wife, Bereswindis, for whose death he was still secretly reproaching himself! This was his daughter; there could be no doubt about it. He was so overcome that all his anger, all his pride seemed suddenly to melt away.

In an uncertain voice he asked, "What have you got in that sack? It looks very heavy for you."

"Bread for my poor. And I must move on again, because they are very hungry."

His child's voice! He could bear it no longer. He jumped to the ground, took Odilia in his arms, and with tears asked her forgiveness.

What celebrations there were at the castle and at Obernai the day Odilia became a princess again! But she herself had only one wish: to remain in the service of God and the poor, to go on living as a nun. She would escape at night from her richly furnished rooms to join her companions, the Sisters, or to visit her beloved poor. And all the money she now received she used to support the hospital and to increase her alms.

Her father, meanwhile, kept repeating, "You have to get married! You are my only child. Who will succeed me if you have no children? Choose anyone you like among the best barons of the country. There are plenty of handsome and valiant young men in Alsace and on the other side of the Rhine who would be glad to marry you. Take your pick."

But Odilia always answered that she had already made up her mind, that she did not want to get married, that she had no desire to become the wife of one of those warriors whom her father kept bringing to her by the dozen, that she had vowed to remain always in the service of Christ. The result was that Adalric grew furious all over again.

One day he announced to Odilia that he had chosen a husband for her himself and that she would have to accept him whether she liked it or not. The wedding, he said, would take place the very next day in the castle.

But that night Odilia ran away. A kind fisherman ferried her across the Rhine in his boat, and she ran off into the thick pine groves of the Black Forest, sure that her father would have sent horsemen in pursuit. Suddenly she heard a sound behind her. It was the steady beat of horses' hoofs. She rushed on, taking the first path she came to. But to her horror, she found that it led to a great rock impossible to climb. She was going to be caught! She turned around, her back to the rock.

Then a miracle took place. Slowly, very slowly, the rock opened. Before the stupefied gaze of Adalric's horsemen, Odilia disappeared, and a spring appeared in her place. The spring, it is said, flows to this day, and the Christians of the Black Forest come there to collect its water.

Odilia came out of the rock without any ill effect, and her father's soldiers escorted her back to the castle with a thousand signs of veneration. But as they arrived in the town of Obernai, they heard the far-off tolling of the passing bell. Duke Adalric had died!

Odilia was in dismay. She bore no ill-feeling toward this man who had been so bad a father. What worried her was that he might have died in a state of rage against her, of violence, of sin. All night long she prayed, in tears, that God might have pity on his soul. And at dawn, Heaven opened and she heard a voice saying, "On your account, because He loves you, the Lord has pardoned your father. Rejoice, for he is saved!"

Her mind at rest, Odilia went back to her beloved convent, where she lived for many long years more. She became abbess and soon had a community of 150 nuns; whereupon she founded a second convent at the foot of the mountain and built more hospitals. Pilgrims flocked from all parts to beg the Saint of Alsace to pray for them. And century after century, even to our own day, people have climbed the mountain that bears the name of the little blind girl whose sight had been miraculously restored by God. And all who go there are certain to find peace and marvelous lessons of faith and charity.

The Boyhood of Louis IX

With shouts of joy, four spirited lads pushed a rowboat onto the clear waters of the Oise River. It was autumn; the fresh wind chased the clouds in the pale-blue sky, rippled the surface of the river, sent the red leaves whirling in the great forests of the Île de France.

"Together now! One, two!" The rowers dipped their oars rhythmically, and the light skiff sped down with the current.

All four boys were around twelve years old, and seeing them in their heavy linen breeches, short tunics, and homespun jackets, all thoroughly soiled from fishing for frogs in the muddy water, you would have thought they were local country lads. But a closer look would have shown that there was something different about them, especially about the tallest of the group, a splendid youngster with long curls, gentle eyes, and delicate features, whom his friends seemed to obey without question. This was none other than Prince Louis, eldest son of the King of France, who would probably be king himself one day, in twenty or thirty years' time.

Twenty or thirty years . . . No, Providence had determined otherwise. Who were those riders cantering along the riverbank, hailing the boat? At first, the boys, absorbed in their rowing, did not hear the shouts.

"One, two! One, two!" The oars continued to beat the peaceful waters. Finally one of them heard the cries. "Stop! They're calling us!"

When they landed, the party of gentlemen on horseback was waiting for them. Prince Louis recognized the Constable of France, the Master of the Horse, the Palace Chaplain, and other high officers of the court. What had happened? Such powerful lords would not have come to him simply to cut short a harmless boat ride. And they all looked so grave and troubled.

Before the Constable could open his mouth, the boy guessed the terrible news. He thought of his father, King Louis VIII, fighting valiantly somewhere in the southern part of the kingdom, having already smashed the English positions. But who can be sure of coming out of a war unscathed?

"The king, my father?" he asked. He had quickly been changing back into the clothes he had left on the riverbank before jumping into the boat: a fine cloth tunic secured with a girdle of silk and gold, and a scarlet cloak lined with gray fur. From the way the gentlemen were bowing before him he knew: King Louis VIII was dead.

The king had died not in battle, but of some strange sickness, an unknown fever — some might say he had been poisoned — as he was passing through Auvergne. He was thirty-six years old. This was the autumn of the year 1226, and the new reign was about to begin.

The boy jumped lightly on the horse that the noble lords had brought him and set off at a gallop. He was eager to reach Poissy with all possible speed, where his mother, Queen Blanche of Castille, must surely be overwhelmed with grief. But when he came into her presence, he did not find her in tears. Her proud Spanish features were strained, ravaged with pain, but not a tear showed upon her face.

The Boyhood of Louis IX

Ever since the black-garbed messenger had brought her the news, she had been praying in the chapel. Prince Louis ran up to her, wanting to throw himself into her arms, like a child. But Queen Blanche made him the ghost of a curtsey.

"My lord," she said in a firm voice, "the king is dead. Now you are the king. From now on, remember your duties!"

∞

Three weeks later, Prince Louis was alone in the chapel of the archbishop's palace at Rheims. It was night, and the darkness was broken only by the flickering flames of the candles. The silence was complete. The law of chivalry required that he who was to be dubbed a knight must spend the whole preceding night alone in prayer, to think upon the obligations he was about to assume.

That evening, the noblest of the knights of France, one of the most valiant warriors of the army, had reminded the young prince of the glory of his family and the examples of his forbears. He had described to him the splendid feats of his father, surnamed "the Lion." He had recalled that in the very year of Louis's birth, 1214, his grandfather Philip (surnamed "Augustus" because he had so greatly enlarged the kingdom) had defeated the formidable coalition of the German emperor and the English king at Bouvines. And the noble knight had also told the boy about those of his ancestors who had been not only great warriors, but also great-hearted rulers, beloved of their people: Louis VI, "who never slept," Louis VII, "the good judge."

Then a priest had gone over the terms of the vow that Prince Louis was to take the following day: to be faithful to God, to obey the law of Christ without flinching, to help the helpless and distressed, to serve justice and truth with all his might. Those were to be his duties at all times. Knighthood was nobility and power placed at the service of the Christian ideal. Louis, throughout his life, was to be a true knight.

The night wore on. The rule forbade him to sit during his vigil. Standing up straight like a soldier, or on his knees like a monk, the boy king prayed. He implored God for the strength to keep his promise, for the grace to be a truly Christian prince. Finally the dawn came, Mass was sung for him, and the ceremony of knighting began. Louis was vested in his coat of mail, and the breastplate was strapped upon him. Then his godfather struck his shoulder with the flat of a heavy sword, saying, "In the name of God, of our Lady, of St. Michael, and of St. George, I dub you a knight. Be always valiant and courteous and faithful." Prince Louis was now a knight.

∞

But this ceremony was to be followed by another, far more solemn and magnificent: Louis's coronation. Queen Blanche, with great political wisdom, insisted that her son should be proclaimed and acknowledged king without any delay whatsoever. For the situation was confused: many great feudal lords, jealous of the royal authority, were ready to revolt. Would they not try to take advantage of this child's minority to avenge themselves for the severe measures that Philip Augustus had taken against some of their number? But once the Church had anointed the new king, making of him a representative of God on earth, it would be more difficult for the haughty nobles to continue their seditious plots and plans.

And so, three weeks after his father's death, Prince Louis was crowned King Louis IX.

The ceremony took place in the white, still unfinished cathedral of Our Lady of Rheims — for this first third of the thirteenth century was just the time when all the great Gothic cathedrals of France were rising from the earth and reaching toward Heaven. Right in the center of the Beauce plain, Our Lady of Chartres was proudly rearing its two spires. In Normandy, the facade of Our Lady of Rouen was completed, but the nave had burned down and had to be started all over again. In Picardy, the best masons were hard at work building the marvel we know as Our Lady of Amiens. And in Paris, the future cathedral of Our Lady of France had been completed as far as the great gallery that was to support the two heavy towers.

A magnificent escort accompanied the boy into the white cathedral of Rheims: princes of the blood, brothers of the king, barons of the highest rank, officers of the court. The archbishop and other prelates greeted him at the entrance and led him to a part of the choir separated from the rest by a door. There a bed had been set up, similar to the beds on which the dead are laid in state, covered with black cloth and surrounded by candles. On this bed Louis lay down.

The archbishop then knocked at the door with an ivory hammer, and the chamberlain replied: "The king is sleeping." The archbishop knocked a second time, and the chamberlain made the same reply. The third time, an officer opened the door, and Louis jumped from the bed and appeared before the assembled company. This symbolic ceremony signified that the crown was immortal, that the royal authority passed from father to son regardless of the individual.

At once the organs broke out in joyous fanfares. The crowd shouted; the bells of Saint-Remy, at the other end of the city, pealed wildly. The great ermine-lined cloak glistening with lilies stitched in gold was placed upon the boy's slender shoulders. He moved forward in the choir toward the archbishop, who was vested in his most splendid robes and surrounded by his chapter, all the dignitaries of the Church and countless priests and religious.

A priest handed the archbishop the Holy Ampulla — the vessel containing the holy oils that an angel was believed to have brought from Heaven when Clovis, the first King of France, was baptized. Taking a little of the sacred oil, the archbishop traced the Sign of the Cross on the boy's forehead, breast, and members. This was to proclaim that the new king must govern his kingdom on behalf of Christ, and in accordance with the law of Christ's gospel. Louis IX — St. Louis, as he was to become — never forgot these obligations.

∞

Now that we have seen him in the splendor of his coronation, in his youthful majesty as the heir to one of the noblest kingdoms on earth, let us look at him as the boy of twelve he still was. His saintly mother, Blanche of Castille, was to go on for many years teaching him how to conduct himself in a manner most fitting to a Christian. For if St. Louis became the model of Christian princes, it was because his mother, all through his boyhood, was the model of mothers and teachers. To his dying day, the great king loved to repeat that he owed everything to the noble lady who had given him more than life itself.

Let us look at St. Louis as he fulfilled all the duties of a well-brought-up child. He applied himself to his studies with joyous zeal. Latin soon became a second language to him, and all his life he loved to read the finest Latin works. He knew the Holy Scriptures, the greatest Fathers of the Church, the lives of the saints, and there was nothing he did not know about the history of his own ancestors. So unusually serious a student was he that — so we are told — if he made the slightest error in his work, he would go to his teacher to be punished; he would kneel down of his own accord to receive the rod.

But what Louis loved most of all was anything that fed his faith. He would spend long hours in church, mingling his voice with the choir as they chanted the Divine Office. Often he would inflict severe penances on himself: for instance, he would fast on bread and water all through Lent. His mother taught him the noblest Christian principles, going so far as to tell him: "If I saw my son desperately sick, and if I could save him by committing a mortal sin, I would rather let him die."

But you must not think that the boy king was brought up like a little monk. Not at all! Blanche of Castille was concerned that her son should display the dignity of kingship even in his bearing and his clothing. Like any other young nobleman of his time, he learned to ride, to fence, to hunt with the hounds, to practice the art of falconry. Every day he spent time training to use arms, for the King of France would always have to be the first soldier in the land.

Imagine, then, a most attractive boy, "gracious and amiable," as one of his confessors described him, loving jokes and fun, but at the same time so grave, so studious, so determined to fulfill his kingly task to the best of his ability. If one of his companions began singing some improper verses in his presence, the young king would mildly reprove him, saying, "You would do better to sing the *Ave Maris Stella*."

One day, when he was asked which saint he admired most, he replied, "St. Francis of Assisi, the meek and joyous saint who died the very year I was born, because he loved poverty above all things." When he went to the Benedictine monastery of Royaumont to attend the Divine Office, the monks at once offered him a place in their stalls. But the king refused and modestly knelt down in a corner of the choir.

On another occasion, he overheard a heated discussion among his ministers: was it worse to have leprosy or to commit sin? Most of them were saying they would rather do anything than have that loathsome disease. Whereupon the young king interrupted them to show them the folly of their argument. Leprosy, he explained, destroyed only the body, which is mortal, whereas sin stains the immortal soul itself.

And here is another scene. At the king's palace in Paris, one hall was set aside for the needy — every day food was served there to anyone who came to beg for alms. About two hundred of them would be there, of every age and sex, not very pleasant to look at with their tattered clothes, their dirt, their vermin — and the smell in the refectory was horrible. Never mind! The young king would very often be there in person to attend the meal of "my lords, the poor."

He would pass between the tables, speak a gentle word to one of the most wretched, examine another's sore and call it to his own doctor's attention, or instruct a servant to help a blind man to eat. Sometimes food would be spilled on his robe, and when it was pointed out to him, he would smile and say, "Never mind, I have others!" Not even the lepers, shunned by everyone because their disease was so contagious, were excluded from his Christian charity. Had not Jesus Himself taught us to recognize His own image in those most disinherited of men? From childhood, St. Louis knew it and was never to forget it.

∞

Your history books will tell you what kind of man St. Louis turned out to be in the course of his glorious reign. They will tell you of a king who always tried to render just judgment to all; a king who showed his Christian spirit by making peace with his defeated enemies; a king who ruled his kingdom with such humanity that, at his death, this popular song could truly express the sorrow of every Frenchman: "The poor, to whom shall they turn now that the good King is dead who loved them so well?" You will learn, too, of his two crusades, and how he died at Tunis, in Africa, lying at his own request on a bed of ashes, and murmuring in his agony, "Jesus! Jesus!"

St. Louis became the man he was chiefly as a result of his upbringing as a child. Without Blanche of Castille, would Louis IX have been a saint? And without the Christian virtues developed in him in childhood, would he have been the model king revered by his whole country?

One day, when the young king — he was about fifteen at the time — was returning from Orleans to Paris, a band of rebel barons tried to seize him. Warned of the plot, the king and his escort managed to reach a fortress where they dug themselves in. A courier was sent to Paris to ask for help.

Queen Blanche immediately had a herald proclaim that her son was in danger. At once the popular militias sprang to arms and the priests rang the alarm bells in all the churches. "God save the king! God save the king!"

The cry rose from every lip and spread from village to village. The whole region was ready to help the king; even the humblest peasants set out with their scythes and pitchforks. Faced with such a reaction, the rebels made off. And when King Louis started out again on the road to Paris, he was accompanied all along the way by his enthusiastic subjects, who were thanking God for saving him from this peril. At fifteen, Louis was already loved as a saint.

~∞~

A Girl of Lorraine

The kingdom of France was truly to be pitied. For nearly a hundred years, it had been torn by invasion and civil strife, and what misery the war had brought upon the country! France, once so fair, so rich, so fertile, was hard to recognize now with its ravaged land, its scanty harvests, its uncertain trade, its deserted roads. Would the English invaders never return to their islands? Would Frenchmen never unite against the common enemy instead of rending each other, divided into the Armagnac and Burgundian factions? Nowhere could people be sure that the next day a band of English or Burgundian troops would not come and set fire to their houses, murder their families, carry off their cattle and plunder the church. And everywhere the talk was only of the misfortunes of the times.

A little girl born near the beginning of the fifteenth century — say, in 1412 — would have heard little else than stories of massacres and disasters since she was first of an age to listen to grown-up talk. She could hardly have understood, at the age of three, what her father was saying when he told of the terrible defeat of the flower of French chivalry and the atrocious massacre ordered by the English king of three thousand of the noblest prisoners. But she would certainly have understood, and never forgotten, what she saw with her own eyes at the age of seven: bitter fighting between hostile groups of Frenchmen, from which many came back badly wounded and many did not come back at all. As a very small child, she would certainly have known by heart the ditty sung all over France:

> Have pity, gracious Lord, our God,
> On France as on other lands!
> Sad it would be beyond bearing
> If the noble realm of France
> Through man's temptation
> Were brought to perdition!

Could there even be said to be a king in the kingdom of France? The poor mad king had been succeeded by ... whom? Some said a little English boy, barely out of his cradle. Others said a sickly youngster, the dauphin Charles, as yet uncrowned and therefore unrecognized as King of France, who lived at Bourges and was more concerned, it seemed, with pleasures than with battles. "Have pity, gracious Lord, our God!"

The great city of Orleans, the last stronghold guarding the Loire and preventing the English from sweeping down on Bourges and the rest of France, had been besieged for months without anyone either wishing or being able to come to its aid.

What, then, could have been sadder, in that year of grace 1428, than "the noble realm of France ... brought to perdition"?

∞

At Domremy, in Lorraine, there lived a girl named Jeanne who had long been thinking of all these things, and her heart ached for her country. She was sixteen, but she looked older. She was tall, strong, with a fresh complexion and a fine carriage. Her clear eyes were full of light. All who knew her described her as pure, wise, very reserved, and wonderfully devout. As for intelligence, this young peasant girl was more than a match for many a scholar.

Domremy was not big — it contained some forty to fifty houses in all — and Jeanne's house was no grander than any of the others. Her parents, Jacques d'Arc and his wife, were honest peasant folk, hard-working, loyal to the Church, like so many others in France in their day. Domremy lay right on the border between the part of France that recognized the dauphin Charles and the part that did not, so its people were particularly well placed to know the horror of war and the urgency of peace. But who would put an end to the war?

The Arc house stood close by the church, and Jeanne went there every day. The bells did not have to call her; she loved to pray alone in the silence of the little nave, over which there always hung a faint odor of incense. She had someone tell her the stories of the saints represented in the statues: St. Remy, bishop of Rheims, who had baptized King Clovis; St. Catherine and St. Margaret, who had died as martyrs because they did not want to deny their faith; and greatest of all, more powerful than the holiest of men, St. Michael the Archangel, leader of the armies of Heaven. It was said he had never been defeated! Indeed, he had just given fresh proof of this: the English who had been besieging Mont Saint-Michel off the west coast of France had been forced to retreat. The rock that bore his name had been saved by its protector!

Jeanne thought, and she prayed. One day, perhaps, the Lord would send someone to clear the land of its invaders, to relieve Orleans, to bring the young dauphin to Rheims to be anointed king. The village gossips often repeated a saying well known all over France: "What a bad woman has done, a wise virgin will undo." The bad woman, without any doubt, was Queen Isabeau, who had deserted her son, the dauphin Charles, and signed a shameful treaty with the English. But who would be the wise virgin?

∞

Jeanne had a secret. She never spoke of it to anyone, not even to her dearest friends, Hauviette and Mengette. Three years earlier, in 1425, an extraordinary thing had happened to her. She had been watching her flocks in the pasture when a storm forced her to take shelter in an abandoned chapel. Had she fallen asleep there? Had she dreamed it all? Yet how clear had been the voice she seemed to hear, telling her, "Go to the dauphin's help!"

Another time, more recently, in the garden near the church, she had seen a great light, and a voice — she was sure it was the same voice — had spoken to her: "I come from God to help you to be good. Be upright and devout; go to church very often, and I will protect you." She had fallen to her knees then, and promised to give herself to God alone and to serve Him her whole life through.

Since then, the mysterious apparitions had often returned: figures such as she had never seen on earth, so beautiful, so dazzling that she could hardly fix her eyes on them. One was like some marvelous bird and at the same time a splendid young man — Jeanne understood that this was St. Michael. At his side were two lovely women with shining faces — these must be her friends of the little church, St. Catherine and St. Margaret, standing there so close to her on the meadow grass or in a clearing of the oak glades. Was she going mad? No, no, it was all true, she was sure of it. The archangel and the two saints came from Heaven to speak to her, and she understood their message.

But she was afraid. In the three years that her heavenly visitors had been coming to her, how often they had repeated the same words! God had heard the prayer of her pure heart. He had pitied the realm of France. He was going to send someone to relieve Orleans, to throw the English back to their islands, to take the dauphin Charles to Rheims to be crowned king. And that someone was to be Jeanne herself!

Jeanne argued, protested. Since when did girls lead armies and win battles? Since when did a peasant girl from Lorraine possess more knowledge and more strength than the king's knights? For days, for months, for three whole years, in fact, she had been struggling, often in tears, while St. Michael commanded and the saints implored her to obey.

Now it was the spring of 1428, and the situation was worse than ever. Orleans, it was said, was completely surrounded. The commander of the English forces, the Duke of Bedford, was boasting that he would soon be master of the whole of France. Jeanne's visitors became ever more urgent, ever more insistent. In the noonday sunshine, in the evening twilight, again and again the supernatural light blazed down on her and the heavenly voices spoke to her. Again St. Michael cried, "Daughter of God, obey! Leave your village and go. In the name of the King of Heaven, raise your standard. Raise it bravely and hasten to battle. God will help you."

∞

Jeanne d'Arc obeyed. She knew exactly what to do; the archangel had instructed her. After so many months of hesitation, of fear, it was sweet and restful simply to be obedient to God. Humbly, she had consented to be an instrument in His all-powerful hands, to throw herself into this amazing adventure, to proclaim in the face of the world that she would lift the siege of Orleans, have the dauphin crowned king of France, and defeat the English.

First, she knew, she had to go to Vaucouleurs, to speak to the captain of the garrison, Robert de Baudricourt. Imagine the scene. Unknown to her parents, there she was at Vaucouleurs, dressed like any other young peasant girl, with nothing to distinguish her from the others. She had needed the support of St. Michael himself to walk through the castle gates, right into the midst of the noisy crowd of knights and soldiers gathered there. Among so many people, she had gone straight up to De Baudricourt, whom she had never seen before, and said, "I am come from my Lord, to ask you to give me armor, a war horse, and a good escort of soldiers, and have me taken to the dauphin of France. For I am commissioned to take him to Rheims to be anointed, once the English are beaten and Orleans has been saved."

De Baudricourt was astonished, to say the least. What could this girl want of him? With her lovely clear eyes, her well-combed black hair and her honest face, she certainly did not look like a madwoman!

" 'My Lord,' did you say? Who is this Lord of yours?"

"He who owns the kingdom of France and all the kingdoms of the earth — the King of Heaven!"

The answer silenced him for a moment. As a good Christian, he was well aware that God could do all things. But in matters like these, would the Almighty make use of this slip of a girl? Like Jeanne herself at first, he felt that it was not a girl's task to lead armies and relieve Orleans.

"Get along with you!" He spoke gruffly, but his tone remained friendly. "Go home to your father. He'll probably give you a sound thrashing to teach you not to tell such stories and come bothering me!"

But hardly had she reached home — and her parents were not very pleased to learn of her escapade — than still worse news came. A troop of English and Burgundians were drawing near and laying siege to Vaucouleurs. It was all De Baudricourt could do to hold his own against them, and deep down he may have thought sometimes of the radiant girl who had told him with peaceful certainty that she had been commissioned to deliver France and restore peace to the land.

Jeanne, meanwhile, was not a bit discouraged at this first failure. The heavenly voices had spoken to her again and consoled her; the supernatural light had enfolded her once more. Now she no longer feared to proclaim her mission out loud. She told Hauviette and Mengette one day: "There is a girl, between Coussey and Vaucouleurs, who will have the King of France anointed within the year." She spoke so firmly and so simply that her friends could not laugh at her. In their hearts they believed her.

Soon all the village was alive with whispers. No one knew what to make of it. Maybe her parents ought to marry her off quickly instead of letting her toy with her daydreams. And here was just the right young man for her! He was saying he wanted to marry her and that she had promised herself to him. Even before the parish priest he insisted that he had received her promise and that he wished to take her for his wife. But to the general dismay, before the priest could come to a decision in the matter, the over-fanciful gallant was found dead! And people began to consider very seriously whether all this was the Devil's handiwork — or God's.

So the summer went by, and the autumn, and now winter had set in. After many weeks of bitter siege, the enemy had had to retreat without taking Vaucouleurs. But the situation remained desperate. Bands of highway robbers, of soldiers separated from their army, were still roving through the countryside of Lorraine, pillaging and burning. The news from Orleans was going from bad to worse: the inhabitants had hardly any food left, and the garrison was exhausted. But the voices continued to sound in Jeanne's ears: "What are you waiting for? Go! Go back to Vaucouleurs! Go to see the captain again . . ." And again she obeyed.

De Baudricourt did not refuse to receive her. Had he been thinking? Had he, too, received some secret call? Very seriously he listened to her as she told him, "Learn, sire, that God has made it known to me many, many times that I am to go to the gentle dauphin and have him crowned King of France. Give me some armed men, and I will go to him; and then, with his army, I will relieve Orleans!"

"Very well, I believe you! I shall write to the king, and if he agrees to receive you, I shall give you a good escort and you can go at your own risk, through many enemy provinces, to speak to him."

While she waited for the dauphin to reply, her story spread. Some believed it, others scoffed. Soon three knights came to her and placed themselves at her service. They had confidence in her; if she left, they would go with her to serve as a guard. But there were others who regarded the whole plan as altogether too fantastic. And these persuaded De Baudricourt to make sure, first, that Jeanne was not a witch. So she was sprinkled with holy water, and requested to go to confession. When these "tests" turned out in the girl's favor, the captain himself was pretty well convinced.

One day she came back to see him. The hour had come, the heavenly voices had announced it. "Delay no longer, sir, in the name of God! For this very day, near Orleans, the dauphin has suffered great harm. If you do not send me to him, he will soon suffer even greater harm."

This was on February 12, 1429. The same day — the news came to Vaucouleurs a week later — the army sent to bring fresh supplies to Orleans had been surprised by the English and cut to pieces.

Then De Baudricourt understood.

∞

Open the city gates! Let this band of warriors through!

See, right there in the midst of those clattering horsemen in their breastplates and helmets and greaves, that slender girl rider dressed as a boy, in black doublet and hose! Her face is radiant with joy and hope, her hand rests on the little sword at her side. She is Jeanne d'Arc, God's messenger riding forth to deliver France, as St. Michael and St. Catherine and St. Margaret had told her.

You probably know what happened after that; it is part of "history" — world history — even though it began in so extraordinary a fashion, almost like a legend. Jeanne, the young peasant girl from Lorraine, made her way across war-torn France to Chinon on the Loire, where she found the dauphin Charles altogether discouraged and unhappy. She gave him proof that she had really been sent by God, with the result that he regained courage and gave her an army to command. With her eight thousand men, Jeanne hastened to Orleans, which the English had been besieging for two hundred days. She forced them to lift the siege and marched in triumph into the city.

A miracle! Could it be that the English were no longer invincible? Their armies kept retreating before the young general. Now Jeanne was able to fulfill the second part of her mission: to take the dauphin to Rheims to be anointed king. The ceremony took place on a fine day in July in the famous cathedral, with Jeanne standing erect near the altar, holding high her white standard embroidered with lilies of gold.

But alas! the king was surrounded by bad counselors. They were jealous of the victorious maiden and prevented her from fulfilling the rest of her mission. As a result, she began to suffer reverses. She was wounded before Paris; at Compiegne, she was captured and handed over to her enemies — Englishmen and false Frenchmen. They proceeded to "try" her, but the trial was an abominable farce. They accused her of being a witch, of having sold herself to the Devil. And when they could not find her guilty, they tried to trap her, exhausted her, tormented her most cruelly in many ways. And finally, in the marketplace of Rouen, they burned her alive. Jeanne, as she died, kept repeating, "Jesus! Jesus!"

For, as you know, Jesus, by His death on the Cross, taught us that nothing great, nothing noble, nothing divine is accomplished save by sacrifice. Jeanne, the maid of Domremy, knew this as soon as she heard the voices of the archangel and the saints.

Aloysius Gonzaga Played Ball

April 20, 1568, was a day of great festivities at the castle of Castiglione, in Lombardy. Hundreds of high-ranking guests thronged the spacious halls and the lovely gardens. The best and richest tapestries hung from the walls; orchestras played at a dozen different points; the fountains in the ornamental lakes rose high and straight, as though to rival the towering cypresses around them.

The occasion for all this rejoicing? The baptism of a tiny baby, Louis, son of the Marquis of Castiglione and of Marta, his wife. The infant whimpering in his lace-trimmed cradle would one day succeed to a fabulous heritage; like his ancestors, he would be a prince of the Holy Roman Empire, Duke of Mantua, a grandee of Spain. He would bear one of the most illustrious names of Italy: Gonzaga.

Gonzaga was a great name indeed, and the family was truly a noble one. Two hundred fifty years earlier, an emperor had rewarded the bravery of a Gonzaga with a princely title and a splendid endowment. Since that day, there was not a generation of Gonzagas that had not distinguished itself in war, in the royal service, or in the Church.

All the princely families of Europe — indeed, all the royal families, too — were related to the lords of Mantua, which explains why so many great personages were gathered at Castiglione on that day for little Louis's baptism. Kings were there, and dukes and cardinals and ambassadors in a dozen dazzling uniforms, among them the ambassadors of His Majesty Philip II, King of Naples and of Spain, for the lady Marta had been both a friend and a lady of honor of Philip's queen, Elizabeth of France.

The rejoicings were perhaps all the greater because everybody knew that there might well have been great mourning instead. When little Louis was born early in March, the doctors had feared not only for his life but also for the life of his mother. And the lady Marta, in that hour of extreme peril, had made two vows to the Blessed Mother: if her child lived and if she herself recovered, she would make a pilgrimage to the Holy House of Loreto, and the boy would be especially consecrated to our Lady. So when the guests at the baptism spoke of the child's future — would he be a valiant soldier, like his father and so many of his ancestors? would he go off to fight in Germany, or France, or even against the Turks? — his mother, in faith and thanksgiving, hoped that her son would be nothing less than a saint.

Louis — or Aloysius, as we call him now — seemed, in fact, destined from earliest childhood to be an altogether exceptional Christian, and at the same time to enjoy God's special protection. As soon as he learned to walk, he would toddle toward the statue of the Blessed Virgin, before which the lady Marta always placed the choicest fresh flowers and kept twelve candles constantly alight. There he would stand, strangely quiet, and look. As soon as he learned to speak, he would recite prayers, and his most familiar words were: "Jesus! Mary!"

Aloysius's pious practices increased both in number and in fervor as he reached the age of reason. So much so, in fact, that the duke, fearing his eldest son might become a monk instead of succeeding him in the government of his estates, would often interrupt him in his prayers, and order a groom to saddle a little horse and take the boy for a good ride in the country to change his ideas.

Although he was so young, Aloysius was already quite clear as to what he must do. He loved to repeat, "What God wants, He does; all we need to do is to trust Him." That trust was well placed indeed. On several occasions, it was obvious that God Himself was protecting him, evidently having special plans for the boy. For instance, when he was five, he was watching a soldier charge a musket. The powder charge suddenly exploded right in the child's face. Everyone thought he must have been burned, disfigured, blinded — but he calmly wiped his face, which bore not the least trace of injury.

Another time, he and his friends were playing with a little cannon that had been given him as a toy. One of the children set fire to the fuse too soon, so that the recoil caught Aloysius right in the chest and knocked him over. Everyone rushed up, thinking him dead, but he simply picked himself up laughing.

Trust, trust in God; to do what Christ wanted and rely on Him for everything — he always gently but stubbornly insisted on these principles. One day he expressed that trust in so lovely an answer that we must set it down here. He was playing ball with some other boys when the chaplain in charge of his religious education came up and asked him, "Aloysius, suppose that at this very moment, someone came to tell you that the world was just about to come to an end, that you were to appear before God, and that you would be judged by the supreme Judge whose verdict would determine how you spent your eternity — what would you do?" A strangely serious question to put to a boy who was skillfully returning a ball to his playmates!

But Aloysius was not at all disconcerted. Calmly and simply as ever, he replied, "Why, I would just go on playing ball!"

A marvelous answer! What better thing could he have done? He knew that from his birth he had always loved and served God to the best of his ability. He had placed all his hope in the Father Almighty. Why, then, should he fear to appear before His face? The chaplain withdrew, marveling at yet another lesson of supernatural trust the boy had given him.

The older Aloysius grew, the more striking his religious and spiritual qualities appeared. When he was eight, he became very gravely ill and suffered much pain. He was so weak that he could not even hold his prayer book. So he would ask his mother, or one of the persons attending him, to read the prayers to him out loud, so that he might at least hear them. At the age of ten, he was already inflicting long penances on himself, remaining for hours before a crucifix, either on his knees or flat on his face on the floor. The vow that the lady Marta had made in his name at his birth, he had secretly repeated in his heart: he would consecrate his whole life to God; he would be a priest of the Lord.

The boy's reputation soon began to spread. Not only within his father's lands, but far beyond, stories were told about the little saint of the Gonzagas. So much so, that one of the most celebrated bishops of the time, Charles Borromeo, Archbishop of Milan, on whom the Pope had conferred the cardinal's hat when he was only twenty-three, and who, throughout his long life, was to be one of the leaders of Christendom, desired to see Aloysius Gonzaga.

The two future saints, the old man and the little boy, were closeted together for quite some time. We do not know what they said to each other, except that — as the archbishop stated later — Aloysius asked as a special favor to be allowed to make his First Holy Communion earlier than was then customary, and the request was granted. And when his father, the Marquis, admitted his displeasure at seeing his eldest son take so little interest in the things proper to his rank, and act in all things more like a little monk, the archbishop told him, "This child will shed greater luster upon the house of Gonzaga than he could have done by force of arms. God has set him apart to be a saint!"

This was a period of tremendous activity within the Church. After the crises caused by Luther, Calvin, and the other "Protestants" who had separated from Rome, the Church, under the direction of her popes, had taken steps to reorganize and defend herself. A great council — that is, an assembly of the most learned clergy of the time — was held at Trent, and its labors, which continued for eighteen years, helped enormously to make Catholic teachings better understood. At Rome, the basilica of St. Peter was being completed, its magnificent dome rising high above the tomb of the apostle. The lovely music of the composer Palestrina was rejoicing the ears and exalting the hearts of the faithful. A few years earlier, in the Gulf of Lepanto, the combined fleets of the nations of Europe had destroyed the Turkish fleet, liberating at one blow more than fifteen thousand Christian captives. How thrilling, then, for a boy to consecrate his life, too, to the glory of the Church, to do his share to further her expansion!

But how? Little Aloysius had not yet decided. Probably he was waiting for the Lord Himself to make clear His commands.

Just half a century earlier, on August 15, 1534, in a chapel on the hill of Montmartre, in Paris, there had taken place a little ceremony that was to have untold consequences. A few Catholics, worried by the progress of Protestantism, had gathered around a priest and pledged themselves to consecrate their lives to the service of souls. Their leader in this resolve was a former officer of the King of Spain, Ignatius of Loyola. After receiving a grave injury on the battlefield, he had spent long months of pain during which he had thought about religion. The result of his reflections was this. The old religious orders, whether contemplative, like the Benedictines, or devoted to preaching, like the Dominicans, were not equipped to combat the new heresies. Something new was needed: a company of men wholly dedicated to the Church and directly subject to the Pope, who would seek, by the example of their lives, and by their teaching and writing and preaching, to make known the true Catholic doctrine.

Pope Paul III had given his approval to Ignatius's ideas, and in 1540, he had authorized the creation of the "Company of Jesus." Its members, the "Jesuits," under the command of their general, were to be like true soldiers in the service of Holy Church — not for nothing had Ignatius been an officer!

The Jesuits had to submit to very strict discipline and under-take long and difficult studies. And so that none should draw any personal glory from his successes, they were constantly shifted around, obliged to live among all kinds of people, both rich and poor, and in the most isolated regions. Their efforts had met with success, and by the time Aloysius of Gonzaga was about sixteen years old, the Company of Jesus was already thriving. The severity of its discipline would hardly have deterred a boy who, at ten, had already been performing penances. It was as a Jesuit, therefore, that he desired to serve God.

One day at Mass, as he was begging the Blessed Virgin to show him what he should do — for he knew that his father would strongly oppose such a step — an inner voice told him, "You are to be a Jesuit." And on November 25 of that year, in 1585, at the age of seventeen, he was admitted to the Company.

Fervor and austerity were common enough in the Company of Jesus, but even there Aloysius stood out by his exceptional devotion and mortification. As he walked through the corridors, his head was always bowed in prayer. At every moment of recreation, he would disappear into the chapel. Although he looked frail and did not enjoy good health, his fasts were rigorous in the extreme, and he continued to punish himself for new faults, even though his confessors could find no fault with him. His mother sent him all the money that belonged to him, but he kept none of it for himself, distributing everything to the poor. No boy of his age could have been more gentle, more simple, more humble, more generous in his charity.

The ancient Greeks and Romans used to say that those who died young were blessed by the gods. Perhaps it is true if one thinks of what so many people do with their lives, of the sum of crimes and sins that pile up in the course of the long years. Aloysius of Gonzaga was to be neither a teacher nor a writer nor a missionary, as he had hoped; God, in whom he had placed all his trust, had decreed otherwise.

During his stay at Naples, he fell sick, recovered, but remained very much weakened. Then an epidemic of plague broke out in the city, not a rare thing in that great Mediterranean port where so many boats put in from the East carrying rats infected with the terrible disease. Aloysius immediately got up from his bed and said that he would go to care for the plague-stricken. His companions did their best to show him that his poor health would make such an undertaking still more dangerous, but in vain. The charity of Christ compelled him, and he obeyed. A few days later, he was struck down, too.

For several days he lay dying, in sublime calm. Why should he fear to stand before Him in whom he had always placed his trust? Was not this the moment to appeal to His kindness, to His mercy? Was not this the moment to go on "playing ball"? His suffering increased, but he did not complain. He asked his brethren to read to him from the works of his favorite saints — St. Augustine, St. Bernard, St. Ignatius. He was so admirable that the representative of the Father General of the Jesuits, who had come to see him, cried out upon leaving him, "Aloysius is a saint — he could be canonized in his lifetime!"

During young Aloysius's last moments on earth, a Jesuit father at his side raised his head a little so that he could see the crucifix better and, in so doing, caused the woolen cap that covered the sick boy's head to slip off. The priest wanted to put it on again, saying, "Brother Aloysius, the evening air might hurt you." But the young saint replied, in a voice as weak as a breath: "Jesus' head was uncovered when He died for us on the Cross."

Those were his last words. A few seconds later, Aloysius of Gonzaga was gloriously entering into that eternal joy to which his hope had led him.

∾

The Lady Spoke to Her

The village of Lourdes lay at the foot of the Pyrenees Mountains in a region at once beautiful and stern. Its people led the simple, hard-working, humdrum existence of so many other villages all over the world, and nothing suggested it would one day become one of the most celebrated spots on earth. The solitary river Gave tumbled its waters over the pebbles, village girls watched their sheep in the pastures, and people were neither better nor worse than anywhere else.

Yet wonderful things were about to happen there. The whole Christian world was to turn its eyes to this poor village, and crowds were to flock there in numbers beyond counting. Why? Because of a very humble little girl to whom the Blessed Virgin had spoken.

∾

On Tuesday, February 11, 1858, at about 9:30 in the morning, three girls — Bernadette and Toinette Soubirous and their inseparable companion, Jeannette Abadie — set out to collect firewood. A little warmth was cruelly needed in the miserable house of the Soubirous family. Toinette and Jeannette walked on ahead, chattering and laughing; Bernadette followed, clutching about her thin shoulders the little hooded cloak a kind neighbor had lent her.

Poor Bernadette — a frail little thing of fourteen who looked no more than ten and plainly didn't get enough to eat! From time to time she would cough, as she always did in winter, and her threadbare clothes were certainly no great protection against the cold. But could you have seen that oval face with the delicate nose and the high forehead, and, above all, those clear eyes, you would surely have said to yourself, "What an engaging child! What a lovely disposition she must have!"

"Come on, do as we're doing! Take your shoes off and wade across," shouted Toinette.

"Lazy! You're letting us do all the work!" called Jeannette, laughing loudly.

To reach the part of the forest where fallen branches could be found, you had to cross a little stream that carried the water from the river to the nearby mill. And since her mother had told her to take care not to catch cold, Bernadette did not want to get her feet wet. So she stayed on the strip of land between the stream and the Gave, alone. Then suddenly —

The most extraordinary thing was happening. She seemed to be caught up in a terrible wind, in danger of being swept away by its force. At the same time, she realized that the still waters of the stream were not so much as ruffled by the wind, and the leaves hung unmoving on the trees. Bewildered, she fell to her knees in prayer.

"Look at her! There she goes again, saying her prayers. That's all she's good for!"

Bernadette started, brought back to herself by her companions' voices. She got up and without hesitation waded across the stream. "Why, the water's warm!" she exclaimed, half to herself.

The two others burst out laughing again, then began shaking her and asking her questions. "What were you staring at just now when you looked like a wax figure?"

Gravely, Bernadette told them: In the cavern that opened on the side of the cliff — the grotto of Massabielle, so it was called — just where a wild rosebush grew, she had suddenly seen an extraordinary light, brighter, more beautiful than any on earth. Then a figure had appeared in the center of the light — a young Lady not over seventeen years old. She was marvelously beautiful and wore a white dress with a blue girdle; her head was covered with a veil that fell about her shoulders. Her hands held a rosary, and each of its beads was like a little light. The lovely Lady's feet rested on a golden rose.

For a moment, the blue eyes had looked upon Bernadette. Then the Lady had smiled and beckoned to her to come nearer. But almost immediately afterward, the wonderful vision had disappeared, the light had faded, and nothing remained but the gray rock and the wild rosebush, stripped of its leaves by the winter frost.

"She's going crazy!" mocked the two girls. "Go tell people your story; you'll see how everyone will laugh at you!"

∞

The Soubirous family, we should explain, were generally regarded in Lourdes as the poorest of the poor. At one time, François Soubirous had owned a mill, but he had been so lazy that business had fallen off, and finally his creditors had forced him to sell. So they had left the old house at the water's edge — father, mother, and four children — with not a penny to their name and no furniture but a bed and a dresser. As they had had nowhere to go, a kind soul had arranged for them to stay in an old prison. The building had fallen into such ruin that it could no longer be used to lock up criminals — but it was considered good enough for the Soubirous family.

The family didn't eat every day. The father worked less and less frequently. From time to time, he would earn a few pennies doing a job no one else would touch: collecting all the unwholesome refuse of the hospital — soiled cloths, bandages, and the like — and disposing of them on a garbage heap at some distance from the village. Not much of a job, as you can readily see, on which to keep a family of six. With the result, so some people said, that Soubirous was not above doing a bit of pilfering. Why, the very winter the Lady appeared, he had been in jail for a few weeks for stealing an old beam he had found lying in the street and cutting off a piece for firewood.

When the tale went around about the strange doings that Bernadette claimed to have witnessed (for, of course, Jeannette and Toinette had not been able to hold their tongues), there was one great guffaw all through the village. "Another Soubirous story!" The girl just wanted to draw attention to herself, although everyone knew she was just a little stupid who hardly knew her ABCs, and who always made a fool of herself by her answers in the catechism class.

As for Bernadette's mother, she did not believe her daughter's story any more than the rest of the villagers did. "You should have waited with your jokes until carnival time!" she told her, furious at hearing the comments of all the village gossips. "If you start again, you'll see what a slap you'll get!"

Bernadette said nothing. She knew that everything she had seen and felt was true. She felt strangely uplifted, in a way she did not understand, as though some secret force were driving her. Why wouldn't people believe her? Had she ever lied? Not that she thought any more highly of herself on account of what had happened. She was so humble that she regarded herself as a poor girl full of faults and weaknesses who certainly had never deserved to be spoken to by a visitor from Heaven. At the same time, if the strange force again drew her to that wild spot, no power on earth would prevent her from making her way there with all possible speed. In her simplicity, she knew that God was calling her.

∞

And the following Sunday, February 14, she heard the call within her. Immediately she ran to the grotto. And everything happened just as before. The same light shone out, the same marvelous figure appeared, smiling at Bernadette and fingering a rosary. Then again the following Thursday, but this time the Lady spoke.

One of the village women, seeing the girl set out on the path leading to the grotto, had run after her with a sheet of paper, intending to write down whatever she might see. But the lovely young Lady told Bernadette, "There is no need to write what I have to say." Then she added, "Will you do me the kindness to come here every day for two weeks?"

"Yes," murmured Bernadette.

And the Lady spoke again: "I do not promise to make you happy in this life, but in the next."

You can imagine how the people of Lourdes greeted these new tales. "That Soubirous child is crazier and crazier," said some. "She should be locked up."

But others began to ask: "And what if it were true? What if this Lady of Bernadette's was a saint — or even our Lady, the Blessed Virgin?"

The place hummed with talk. No one else either saw or heard the things the girl described. All the onlookers saw was Bernadette kneeling in the meadow grass, her arms outstretched as on a cross, her face strangely pale, her fixed gaze seeming to behold some invisible presence. Only her lips moved, as though in prayer, but nobody could catch the words.

After that, every day, in obedience to the command she had received, Bernadette went back to Massabielle. And every day the Lady appeared. And every day, when Bernadette came out of her trance, she would tell what she had seen and heard. Once she said that the Lady had taught her a prayer for herself alone which she was to say silently until her death. Another time, she said that the Lady had appeared to her with an extremely sad expression and commanded her, "Pray for poor sinners!" And still another time, when the little girl was at prayer, reciting the Rosary, which she always brought with her now, she suddenly fell to the ground in sobs. She kissed the earth, crying, "Penitence! Penitence!" then she straightened up again, her face alight with joy.

How strange it all was! But what happened the morning of February 25 was stranger still.

Bernadette was praying before the grotto, as usual on her knees. Suddenly she arose with a bewildered air and looked about her on every side. Then she fell down again and began scraping the earth with her nails. A puddle of muddy water appeared. Bernadette put her face into it. What was that? She seemed to be eating that mud mixed with grass. And the people around began to shout, "Enough, enough! She's crazy! Lock her up!" Some of them rushed up to her, lifted her up bodily, and carried her home.

"You crazy child!" her mother cried, too. "Why did you do that?"

And Bernadette replied, "The Lady told me to. She said to me, 'Go, drink at the spring and wash in it, and eat of the grass you will find there.' " So she had obeyed.

But that afternoon, a rumor began to spread through Lourdes. At the place where Bernadette had scraped the ground with her nails, a spring had appeared. First a trickle of water, then a real little stream that soon had to be channeled with a tree trunk. That evening, the whole village gathered there and noted with amazement that the flow of the spring had considerably increased. By the very next day, it was producing twenty-five gallons a minute, or thirty-six thousand gallons in twenty-four hours. It was the famous Lourdes spring, now celebrated throughout the world, where the sick go to bathe and pray to God to cure them.

Only a week later, there was a new sensation in the village. A blind quarryman named Bourriette had someone bring him a little bottle of water from the new spring. He had rubbed his eyelids with it and at once regained his sight. Rushing to the doctor, who had vainly been treating his eyes for years, he cried out, "A miracle, a miracle! I can see!"

Everyone was asking Bernadette the same question: Who was this Lady? Was she a saint? An angel? Couldn't Bernadette ask her?

Finally, on March 25, the feast of the Annunciation, she gave an answer. Yes, the Lady had told her. She had said, "I am the Immaculate Conception" — that is, the one who was born free of all fault, of all stain; the one whom God wanted free of all sin, even of Original Sin, because of her would be born Jesus, the Savior of the world. The Blessed Virgin Mary — that was the wonderful Lady who had appeared to Bernadette!

∞

More excitement, more heated talk!
"Miracles! We're seeing miracles!"
"No, no, it's all fake, lies!"

"But they are miracles, they are. It was our Lady herself. Hasn't Bourriette been cured?"

"I tell you your Bernadette is crazy!"

"And I tell you she's a saint! Why, when she was praying before the grotto, she put her hand on a lighted candle and there wasn't a trace of a burn!"

"That just goes to prove she's afflicted with a nervous disease."

And so it went.

Each time, now, that Bernadette went to the grotto, hundreds and even thousands of people followed her, hoping to behold the mysterious presence. It was even necessary to throw little bridges across the millstream. In fact, the police had to come to keep order.

The district attorney made an inquiry and himself questioned the girl. The newspapers of the whole region were full of the strange happenings; indeed, they were full of a great deal of nonsense on the subject. Finally the government in Paris grew alarmed at the uproar that was going on in this remote little spot in the Pyrenees.

In the midst of all the commotion, Bernadette herself remained perfectly composed. She was not in the least bit proud at finding herself the center of attention. She continued to lead the humble existence of the very poor. She prayed a great deal; she was always saying her Rosary. All these people questioning her, these serious gentlemen, these doctors — it wearied her, but it did not upset her. She had her inner force to sustain her, that voice which was telling her to stand firm.

Finally, on July 16, Bernadette went to Massabielle once more. But she found her beloved little spot very much changed. Orders had come from Paris to put a stop to the whole business. The mayor had sent a band of workmen to put a high fence around the little meadow in front of the grotto. Bernadette could no longer go in.

She came near the barrier and stood on tiptoe. Immediately the crowd — for a crowd had followed her — cried out, "The Virgin is there!"

Bernadette had fallen into a trance again. With intent gaze, full of love and fervor, she looked upon the invisible. Her lips moved; she seemed at the height of joy. After a long while, she turned round. "The Lady bade me farewell," she said. "She will not come back anymore."

And that was, in fact, the last of the apparitions. But not the end of this marvelous story. Soon the whole world knew it. Soon in all Catholic churches it was rumored that the Blessed Virgin had appeared to a little girl and had spoken to her.

Now it was no longer merely the curious who came to Lourdes, but thousands of pilgrims. Many sick people wanted to wash in the waters of the miraculous spring. The public authorities were aroused; the religious authorities were concerned.

In the autumn of 1858, the Bishop of Tarbes decided to send a commission of priests to Lourdes to examine Bernadette. They questioned her at length. Again and again they asked her about what the Lady had told her. Their conclusion was that Bernadette was a very good child, pure, innocent, and perfectly faithful to the teachings of the Church.

Meanwhile the miracles continued. Sick people, it was said, had been cured, the paralyzed had been able to walk again, the dying had been restored to health.

Finally, after three years of reflection and investigation, the Bishop of Tarbes solemnly declared that the apparitions at Lourdes had been true: the Blessed Virgin had really appeared to Bernadette Soubirous.

What a triumph for her! Would it not go to her head? On the contrary. Just as the whole world was saying she was a saint, she was leaving Lourdes. She was asking to be admitted to a convent of the Sisters of Charity.

The Superior was expecting an extraordinary girl, perhaps one visibly illuminated by the glory of the apparitions. So when she saw the simple little peasant girl, she could not help exclaiming, "What! Is that all!"

And Bernadette, laughing heartily, replied, "Why, yes, that's all!" Then she added, "What does one do with a broom after it's been used? One puts it away in a corner, behind a door. Well, Reverend Mother, I was just a broom, an instrument in God's hands."

Was that not the true language of humility, the very voice of sanctity?

≈

The Young Martyrs of Uganda

"No, I will not betray the promises I made at my baptism! No, I will not go back to worshiping idols and fetishes! No, no, I would rather die!"

What century are we in? Are we back in Rome, at the time of the great persecutions? And this boy who is boldly proclaiming his faith, is he a brother of St. Agnes or St. Blandina? No, we are near the end of the nineteenth century. And where? Let us see.

The boys are young, fourteen or fifteen years old. There are about forty of them, lined up next to one another in bamboo cages, their necks secured in a kind of halter, one foot and one wrist pinned down by heavy pieces of wood.

Dozens of monstrous figures are leaping about before them: faces smeared with red clay and streaked with soot, heads bristling with feathers, animal skins around their hips, bone necklaces clanking against their chests, and little bells tinkling against their ankles. They are sorcerers. But their threatening gestures, their shrieks, their savage chants do not shake the courage of these young heroes of Christ any more than does the sight of the huge pyre being prepared nearby.

They all died, without a moment of weakness, without a single one deserting and betraying the Faith. This story of the young martyrs of Uganda is one of the most splendid stories in the splendid history of the Church. Here it is.

∞

Christianity has come to the immense "Dark Continent" of Africa chiefly during the past hundred years. It has been brought by those admirable people, the missionaries — priests and monks of boundless devotion, unfailing courage, marvelous goodness. Their courage as they have pushed forward through hostile territories among still savage peoples is matched only by their patience and their gift for organization. Once they have settled among the natives, they have brought them not only the teachings of Christ but also aid of every kind.

The missionaries, indeed, have been the truly peaceful conquerors of Africa; without arms, they have won huge lands for civilization. Today there is no region, however distant, however remote, without its missionaries. The natives come to the Father for everything: for advice, for medicine, for protection. If the Church now has thousands of faithful on the "Dark Continent," the credit for it goes to the missionaries.

Foremost among these apostles of recent times have been the White Fathers. They were founded by a man of genius, Cardinal Lavigerie, for the express purpose of teaching the gospel in Africa. The Fathers were to live the life of the natives, dress like them, speak their tongue. They were to be aided by the White Sisters, who would live in the same way and care especially for the women and children. "A hundred million human beings are out there waiting for Christ. I want to give them to Him!" Cardinal Lavigerie once exclaimed before Pope Pius IX. Faithful to that promise, the White Fathers and White Sisters have ever since labored tirelessly to make it come true.

The Young Martyrs of Uganda

Round about 1880, the White Fathers entered Uganda. Let us find Uganda on the map. Look at East Africa, south of the Sudan and Abyssinia. There lies an immense tableland dominated by the great volcanic mountain mass of Elgon. A magnificent body of water — Lake Victoria, so vast that little tides form in it — covers the southern part, and from this lake flow two rivers that eventually come together to form the Nile. This high plateau with its temperate climate and sufficient, but not excessive, rainfall is quite rich and fertile. Bananas, coffee, maize, and sugar, as well as sheep and cattle, provide the people with a good livelihood.

Eighty years ago, the people of Uganda (known as Bantus), like practically all the natives of Africa, were fetishists — that is, they worshiped crude idols carved in wood, numerous gods to whom they made bloody sacrifices. At the same time, the Arabs along the coast were trying to win them for Islam, or the religion of Mohammed. The Christian missionaries, therefore, had no easy task before them.

Yet they were astonishingly successful. After less than five years of work by the missionaries, extremely fervent groups of Christians had formed in many districts of Uganda. In some villages, the Christians numbered 250 or more. And every month their numbers grew. Even before they were baptized themselves, the catechumens — those receiving religious instruction — would spread the Good News among their relatives and friends, and every one of them would bring along another recruit.

Soon there were Christians even at the court, where boys from the best families served the young King Mwanga as pages. The principal page was Charles Lwanga, and when he became a Christian, many of the others followed suit. The king was still a fetishist, but right under his nose, so to speak, Christian ceremonies were being celebrated with faith and fervor.

Now, the king was a violent young man given to fits of rage. At the same time, he was easily influenced by others, and those who enjoyed his confidence could make him do practically whatever they pleased. The man he trusted most was his prime minister, who hated Charles Lwanga and the Christians. This man missed no opportunity of telling the king that the missionaries were really agents sent by the whites to undermine his power; if he let them go on with their work, he would soon find his country invaded by the English and the French and the Germans. Meanwhile the Arab traders to whom the people of Uganda sold their produce were telling Mwanga that he would do well to embrace the religion of Mohammed.

At first Mwanga hesitated. Then one day he announced that he was going to make Mohammedanism the compulsory religion of all his subjects. At this, one of the White Fathers living in the country bravely presented himself before the king and demanded that all the people of Uganda be permitted to worship God as they pleased. He was successful. Mwanga did not dare defy the white men directly, for fear some European nation would send an expedition against him. However, he continued to nurse his anger at those of his own people who had received baptism. And one day the storm broke.

∞

In the autumn of 1885, in an outburst of fury, the king ordered that one of his advisers, Joseph Mkasa, a Christian, be burned alive. As the martyr was dying, he spoke these wonderful words echoing those of our Lord on the Cross: "Go and tell Mwanga that I forgive him with all my heart and that I urge him to mend his ways."

But this outrage, far from frightening the Christians, only served to heighten their courage. The situation became so grave that before the White Fathers would administer baptism to anyone requesting it, they would warn him that he was risking his very life and must reflect seriously before receiving the sacrament. But the number of baptized kept growing just the same, and growing very fast.

Among the pages, there was a positive rivalry as to which would prove himself the best Christian. Groups of these young people, to whom Charles Lwanga had spoken about Christ and the truths of the Faith, were constantly coming to the missionaries and asking to be baptized. The memory of their martyr, Joseph Mkasa, confirmed them in their decision. At one time, twenty-two were baptized; at another, fifteen. Finally nearly all the king's pages were Christians.

The king knew about it, of course. One day, as he was passing the pages in review, the little tyrant cried out, "Let those who do not pray with the white men step forward!" Only three stepped forward. All the rest had either been baptized already or were resolved to seek baptism.

The king went into one of his own special rages. He ordered the prime minister to shut all the boys up in a camp, well guarded by soldiers, until he should have decided what to do with them. And he began yelling, "I must get rid of all these villains who want to dethrone me! I must kill them all!" And as one of his sisters pleaded for mercy for the pages, he seized one of them and killed him with his own hand.

For many long months, the pages were kept in a concentration camp, barely fed, constantly threatened. Every day they were told they would be tortured, burned alive, torn to pieces, thrown to the beasts. Not one of them wavered. Behind their bamboo bars they went on praying together, and their great leader, Charles Lwanga, baptized four who had not received the sacrament before their arrest.

When the king learned of this, his exasperation passed all bounds. He called his council and announced that the young pages who insisted on remaining Christians must die. He spoke so threateningly, in fact, that even the parents of most of the pages began to cry out in terror: "Kill them, O king! Kill these ungrateful and rebellious children. We will give you others."

"Let them all die!" shouted the king.

But even faced with the threat of imminent death, not one of the pages fell away. All of them declared they would rather be tortured and killed than deny their Faith. Among them was a fourteen-year-old lad named Mbaga, the son of the chief executioner. His father offered to help him escape, and his mother implored him to say that he no longer prayed with the whites. But he still refused.

They were marched in fetters and chains to a place in the midst of the forest some thirty-seven miles from the capital — probably for fear the sight of all these young victims might arouse the people and touch off a revolt. Those who proved too weak for the long trek, those who fell, those whose ankles swelled were killed on the spot with a thrust of the spear. At night they were even more tightly bound, enclosed in bamboo cages. As though they had any desire to escape! They kept singing hymns, and three who had been able to escape returned of their own accord to rejoin their comrades.

When they came to the place of execution, and stood in full view of the huge pyre on which they were to be burned alive, they were again urged to deny their Christian Faith. All of them refused.

"Then you can be roasted, to see if your God is strong enough to deliver you!" cried one of the executioners.

And one of the young pages, Bruno, calmly replied, "You can burn our bodies. But you will not burn our souls. Our souls will go to Paradise."

Then the ghastly ceremony began. One by one, the martyrs were wrapped in mats of reed, and the living fagots were placed on the pyre. When Mbaga's turn came, his father, the chief executioner, could not face seeing his child burned alive, so he took him aside and struck him down with a club. Then a flame shot out, and great shouts and songs of thanksgiving mingled with the frantic beating of the tom-toms as the native sorcerers danced around the pyre. The little martyrs of Uganda had given their lives for Christ.

Thus the days of heroism are not ended in the Church. And just as in the old days, when Christians died in the amphitheaters of Rome, children have given us an example in our own times.

You remember the Christian writer of the fourth century who said, "The blood of martyrs is the seed of Christianity"? Wherever there have been martyrs, the good seed has truly grown and magnificent harvests have been reaped. So it has been in East Africa, where the young saints of Uganda have interceded in Heaven for their kinsmen, and their prayers have been heard. Today in Uganda, out of a population of two million, about six hundred thousand have been baptized, and a native clergy and native Sisters are working hard to convert the rest of their brethren. There you see the power of example, the lesson of sacrifice. The blood of the heroic pages, here as everywhere, has truly been the seed of Christianity!

∞

Dominic Did Nothing Out of the Ordinary

Do you know the city of Turin? Everyone knows it by name, of course. It is the capital of Piedmont, a famous province of Northern Italy, and a great center of commerce and industry. About a hundred years ago, it produced the political movement — the *Risorgimento*, or resurgence — which united the warring Italian states into a single nation under the leadership of the princes of Piedmont, the House of Savoy.[2]

Visitors to Turin find it beautiful, with its well-planned streets bordered by high arcades that give it an air of unusual dignity. From the top of the hill overlooking the city, where the great Basilica of Superga stands, you can see the snow-capped Alps rising majestically over the horizon. A lovely city indeed!

But Turin has still another claim to our admiration — I mean to the admiration of Christians. In the nineteenth century, it was not only a political capital with a splendid future before it; it was also a capital of holiness. There is no doubt that in all Catholic Europe there was no other city where lived so many holy people later to be canonized by the Church. Yes, by a singular chance — or the

[2] So called because these princes originally came from Savoy, which is now a province of France.

intention of Providence — there were in Turin an amazing number of men, of women, and even, as you will see, of children who had only one thought: to serve God by carrying out His commandments and devoting themselves to the task of helping the unfortunate.

It would be impossible to name them all — that would take far more than the few pages of this chapter. But we should at least mention Don Cafasso (*Don* in Italian is the title given to a priest in Italy), who spent his life helping prisoners and assisting those who were condemned to death. And also Don Cottolengo, who was so moved when he saw a poor woman dying of cold and hunger because no hospital would take her in, that, without any money, he founded a hospice for the relief of every form of human misery. Today it has become the marvelous "city of charity" in Turin, sheltering no fewer than eight thousand persons.

Of all these saints of Turin, the most celebrated, of course, is Don Bosco — the very appealing St. John Bosco — one of the most extraordinary saints of his own time and indeed of any time. As a young priest, he was horrified to find large numbers of homeless boys roaming the streets of Turin like so many stray dogs, without families, without food, without shelter. He began by taking one boy to live with him, then two, then a dozen, then dozens more. That was the beginning of the Oratory of St. Francis of Sales, where the orphans, or abandoned boys, were not only received, housed, and fed, but also educated and prepared for life.

A congregation of priests was to grow up around the good Don Bosco, to help him and to further his work — these were the Salesian Fathers — and also a congregation of Sisters, to do the same work among girls. Don Bosco was always glad and cheerful, delighting to play with his boys, unequaled in performing magic tricks and climbing a greased pole! He was also unequaled as a teacher; his authority was smiling yet firm, and no one knew better than he how to be a leader of men — and of children.

∞

One day toward the end of October 1854, a little boy rang the bell of the Oratory of St. Francis of Sales. He was a skinny little fellow with big, gentle blue eyes that seemed to fill his thin, pale face. He had just got off the old stagecoach drawn by four horses which had jolted him all the way from Castelnuevo to Turin. He had crossed the whole city, gazing with astonishment at the crowds, at the number of carriages in the streets, at the beautiful things in the shop windows, at the variety of displays in the marketplace.

In a voice that trembled a little, he told the porter, "I am Dominic Savio. I have come from Castelnuevo. I should like to see Don Bosco. I believe he is expecting me."

Don Bosco was, in fact, expecting him and gave him a warm welcome. Little Savio's shyness did not take long to melt away. When Don Bosco looked at you with those laughing eyes of his, you couldn't help being at your ease. From the very start, Dominic felt complete trust in this priest who from now on was to take the place of his own father.

He looked at Don Bosco and then at the Latin inscription behind him. "What does that mean?" he asked.

Don Bosco explained: "It is what I ask God every day: Give me souls, and keep all the rest!"

"Oh," said the boy gravely, "it's a soul trade that you're carrying on here? You buy souls for Heaven. I hope mine will be bought, too."

And Don Bosco replied with smiling seriousness, "That depends only on you, Dominic."

As he said this, he was considering the boy carefully. Dominic did not look the twelve years marked on his baptismal certificate;

he seemed so delicate, so frail. And yet a singular force came from him, a spiritual force. Don Bosco was not surprised at this, anymore than at the boy's answer. His friend Don Cafasso, also a childhood friend of the blacksmith Savio, Dominic's father, had told him something about the boy.

Even as a very little child, Dominic Savio, guided by his saintly mother, had loved above all things to go to church. At the age of five, he had persuaded Don Zucca, his parish priest, to teach him to serve Mass, even though he was so small that his head did not reach as high as the altar. So exceptional was the child's piety that when he was seven, his parish priest told him he would let him make his First Communion — an almost unheard-of thing at a time when children did not make their First Communion before twelve years of age. At school, Dominic had been not only an earnest student, but also a model classmate, preferring to be punished himself rather than tell on another boy. When he was asked why he let himself be accused unjustly, he admitted that he had thought of our Lord Jesus Christ, who allowed Himself to be unjustly condemned.

Don Bosco knew all this. He looked affectionately at the thin little boarder sent him from Heaven. "Go and play with the other boys," he told him.

But perhaps he also knew — for he knew so many things hidden from ordinary men, and he was even said to be able to read souls like an open book — that the Oratory of St. Francis of Sales had received its first saint.

∞

If he had any doubts in the matter, Dominic's conduct and speech would speedily have cleared them away. For scarcely had little Savio entered the Oratory and become a student among the rest than it became quite clear that he was not at all like the others. Not that he was sad or surly or unable to join in the others' play. On the contrary, to the extent his size and poor health permitted, he took part in their games and was one of the most eager players on the ball and bowling teams. But he possessed a kind of mysterious authority over the others, even the roughest and toughest, and Don Bosco knew well enough the reason for this strange prestige.

One day, Dominic came to Don Bosco and said to him, "Father, in your sermon this morning, you said that God was asking us all to become saints. Deep down inside me, I feel the need to be a saint. Tell me how to set about it. By myself I might take the wrong road."

Don Bosco answered, "It's quite simple; all that's needed is that you do your duty, your whole duty, joyfully, for God."

And that is exactly what Dominic Savio did in the three short years he spent at the Oratory. Outwardly, he did nothing out of the ordinary. He was a good student, but there were other good students. He was a good companion, but there were other good companions. The boys at the Oratory got along well together, and even if quarrels broke out, they did not last.

Don Bosco was a master at training his boys to be generous, unselfish, willing. The people of Turin had good proof of this when a cholera epidemic swept the city and the Oratory lads came forward as volunteers to assist the sick and even to help bury the dead. Yet even here Dominic soon stood out as more unselfish, more friendly than the rest. And he went oftener, too, to the chapel, where he could be found praying for hours on end.

What Dominic Savio did among his schoolmates came to light only later, when everyone began to tell what they knew about him. Once he asked a boy to come into the chapel with him. The boy refused, saying it was too cold there and his hands were already covered with chilblains. Without a word, Dominic took off his woolen gloves and handed them to him.

Another time Dominic organized a quiz game; the winner was to get a prize — one of his own possessions — and the subject of the quiz was the catechism. Again, when a bully punched him right in the face, instead of trying to return the blow or report the boy, he spoke to him so kindly, so lovingly, that the other broke down and cried. He promised to resist his violent instincts, and he kept his promise.

Still another time, happening to arrive just as two of his schoolmates were about to fight each other with slingshots, Dominic threw himself between the two, crying, "I want the first stone to be for me!" And the others had not dared shoot.

Thus, Dominic Savio's presence in the Oratory was enough to make the atmosphere even more friendly, more loving — in other words, more Christian. A little group even formed around him that he called the Company of the Immaculate; each member promised to pray often and to live like a true child of the Blessed Virgin.

∞

But, alas, there was one thing that was not going well in little Dominic's life — his health. From month to month it grew worse. Tuberculosis, which modern medicine is able to fight and cure, was then a dreadful scourge; practically nothing could be done against the "chest sickness," as it was called. Dominic coughed more and more; he grew thinner and paler each day. What was to be done? Don Bosco had to consider the others; tuberculosis is most contagious, and to keep the sick boy among all these lads would be very dangerous. Finally, with a very heavy heart, the superior of the Oratory decided to send Dominic home to his family.

The person who took the painful decision most calmly was Dominic himself. He knew perfectly well what it meant; in fact, he called together his friends of the Company of the Immaculate to bid them farewell and asked their prayers for him as for one already dead. Then he went back to his own village. There his condition grew rapidly worse. His distracted family called in the doctor, but as we have said, in those days there was no remedy for tuberculosis. All the doctor did was to follow an old-fashioned method of treatment and to bleed the frail lad again and again. Already Dominic had little enough strength — yet he was bled ten times in four days!

The fifteen-year-old Dominic bore this final ordeal with a courage that many an adult might have envied. After bleeding him the tenth time, the so-called doctor exclaimed, "Now the sickness has been overcome!"

Dominic burst out laughing. "The world has been overcome!" he exclaimed weakly. "Now all that remains is to cross the threshold of eternity."

He crossed that threshold with his customary calm and simplicity. When he felt the end was near, he asked his father to open his missal at the prayers for the dying and read them to him. He made all the responses, without missing a word. His poor mother, meanwhile, unable to bear the scene, had rushed out of the room and was sobbing her heart out on the stairs. The father's last memory of his son was seeing him raise himself on his sickbed, his face suddenly rested and glowing, and hearing him murmur, quite clearly: "It's beautiful, what I see . . ."

∞

What Dominic saw as he passed into eternity he must certainly already have glimpsed during his short life. Of course, he had never boasted of having visions or ecstasies like some of the great saints. But later, when recollections of him were assembled, those who had known him or in whom he had confided told of astonishing graces he had received; indeed Heaven itself had often been present to him in his daily life.

Once, when he was only five years old, he had walked a long distance alone and was almost exhausted. A shining young man had picked him up in his arms and carried him to the doorstep of his home, then had disappeared. Another time, as he was trudging along wearily by himself, he met a "lovely Lady" who kept him company, but she also vanished as he reached his destination.

Another incident of this kind occurred when he was at the Oratory. One day, when everyone was looking for him, thinking he had disappeared, Don Bosco found him in a corner of the chapel. Dominic had been praying there for seven whole hours, and had completely lost track of the time. His eyes were turned to the altar; his face was alight as though he were seeing things ordinary mortals cannot see.

No sooner, then, had Dominic died, than a real "golden legend" sprang up around his gentle person, but a legend in which the facts were true, known, and checked. It was recalled, for instance, that one day he had gone to knock at the door of a house in Turin, saying a sick person was there in danger of death and that a priest must be called at once. At first, those who opened to him had simply laughed at him, but upon making a thorough search of the house, they had discovered an old cleaning woman dying in an attic. It was also recalled that one day Dominic had asked Don Bosco's permission to go home to his village, because he knew his mother was very ill. "Have you had a letter?" Don Bosco asked him. "No," Dominic replied, "but I know it." And it had been true. Don Bosco, in any case, could not doubt that his little pupil had received extraordinary graces, for several years after his death, Dominic appeared to him, clothed in a tunic of dazzling white, and spoke to him of the joy which is the lot of the just in Heaven.

Such was Dominic Savio, the little boy who seemed to have done nothing out of the ordinary. The Church wanted all the boys in the world to know his story and to follow his example. That is why in 1950 she declared him "Blessed," and in 1957, exactly one hundred years after his death, proclaimed him a saint.

St. Dominic Savio, model of Christian schoolboys, pray for us!

⚭

"Let the Little Children Come to Me"

In every century, then, and in every country where the Cross has been planted, we find wonderful witnesses to Christ among children who have lived in obedience to His commandments and died in His love. In the chapters we have just read, you have met a few such figures selected from a multitude. The striking thing is not that children and young people should have been able to give such splendid examples to their fellow Christians, but that there should have been so many of them.

We have told the stories of St. Agnes and St. Blandina, but we might equally well have written of a host of others. There was St. Catherine, for instance, a wealthy young Egyptian girl of Alexandria, who at eighteen was renowned for her learning. At that time, there was a persecution of Christians and she heard that a number of them, terrified at the prospect of torture, had denied their faith and consented to worship idols. Immediately she went to them, exhorted them to return to their faith, brought many back, and was then herself arrested. She died a martyr together with the rest.

Or there was St. Margaret, the daughter of a heathen priest of Antioch, who had been baptized by her nurse and who refused, despite the most frightful torture, to betray her faith. Or St. Christina, a little Italian girl of twelve, who broke the idols in her father's house, gathered the gold that adorned them and gave it to the poor; she, too, was to die a martyr, after God had repeatedly and miraculously saved her life. Or St. Eulalia, a young Spanish girl, also twelve years old, who joyfully died a martyr's death for a similar offense.

The period of persecutions, that is, the first four centuries of our era, was full of such figures — young people who shed their blood for Christ with a courage that many adults could not have mustered. One would like to list them all, but that is impossible because there were too many. But let us at least mention the seven sons of St. Felicitas — Januarius, Felix, Philip, Silvanus, Alexander, Vitalis, and Marcellus. All were arrested, together with their mother, and exhorted under pain of torture to sacrifice to idols. Felicitas was present, but her great fear was not that she might see them die before her eyes but that one of them might weaken. But not one of them did; not one of them betrayed the Faith. And one after the other, they suffered all the most cruel tortures their tormentors could devise. Their mother died last, "having" — to quote St. Gregory — "suffered death eight times, seven in her sons and once in her own body."

∞

But the period of persecutions was not the only one to produce heroic young Christians like these. As you learned when you read the story of the young pages of Uganda, children have been witnesses to Christ, to the point of sacrificing their lives, right up to the most recent times. Indeed, any Christian may be faced with the choice of dying for his faith or denying it, and it is a choice for which he should be prepared beforehand.

Most of us, however, are not required to die as martyrs but to live as true Christians. And that is perhaps even harder! This is the reason that, over the centuries, the Church has canonized men and women who have shown themselves from their youth absolutely faithful to the law of the Lord and have lived in Him. Here again, what a list we would have to make if we wanted to include them all! The thing that strikes us in the lives of the saints is that so often there does not appear to have been anything unusual about them. It was the simple, humble virtues of every day that made them saints.

Take, for example, that young Jesuit, St. John Berchmans, who lived in Belgium at the beginning of the seventeenth century. If you wanted to set down the story of his life, you would find very little to say. There were no sensational events, no startling miracles. We know simply that from earliest childhood, he loved to spend hours in prayer; that when he was twelve, he announced his vocation to the religious life; that upon entering the Society of Jesus,[3] he stood out by reason of his industry and piety; and that he died when he was only a little over twenty, showing marvelous trust in God. Nothing very dramatic, as you see, but you know yourselves how difficult it is to be only the least bit hard-working, obedient, and faithful to God's law, so perhaps you can understand how these very simple virtues can make saints.

And what about that little French girl Thérèse of Lisieux, now probably the most honored woman saint in the world? She left her father's house only to enter the convent of Carmel, where she spent the rest of her life without anything out of the ordinary appearing to disturb her daily routine. But in the depths of her soul, she discovered a love of Christ so strong, so sublime, that it literally devoured her, so that she died at the age of twenty-four. There was little enough excitement in her life either.

[3] That is, the Company of Jesus, or the Jesuits.

Golden Legend of Young Saints

∞

That is the saints' real lesson for us. The wonders that some have worked, the miracles that have often marked their lives — and even more often have occurred after their death, at their intercession — are assuredly very important, manifesting as they do God's glory. But what is far more important is the example so many of the saints have given of quiet, simple lives, hardly any different, so it would seem, from our own, but wholly, magnificently, dedicated to the Lord.

Holiness does not mean living differently from others; it does not mean that we have to leave everything and shut ourselves up in a cloister, or that we have to face ravenous lions on the sand of an arena. It is both much simpler than that, and very difficult. It means this: to act as Christians wherever God has placed us; to cultivate those virtues which make us feel at peace with God.

One can be a perfect Christian in the midst of the greatest riches, and even on a throne like St. Louis, whose story you have read, or others we could have mentioned — for instance, St. Henry, the German Emperor, or St. Elizabeth of Hungary. But one can also be a saint in utter poverty, and not necessarily by giving up everything like the "little poor man" of Assisi, St. Francis. Some of us need only to live in our own families and accept the fact of being of humble background and of having nothing. St. Benedict Labre did not come of well-to-do people; he became the "beggar pilgrim" and lived without possessing anything but the miserable bowl with which he begged a little soup from door to door. The family of St. Jean-Marie Vianney was also poor; he entered the seminary through the charity of others and became that model of all parish priests: the Cure d'Ars.

"Let the Little Children Come to Me"

In recent years, the Church has held up several children as models for the faithful. We have just read about St. Dominic Savio, and we have seen that his life was just as uneventful, outwardly, as that of St. John Berchmans. It was the simple, humble virtues that brought them both to glory. Another child saint, whose story is certainly more dramatic, in fact teaches us the same lesson. Her name was Maria Goretti, and she lived at the turn of the century in the region of the Pontine Marshes, in Italy. Life there was extremely hard; the soil was poor and there was much disease. At eleven, Maria helped her widowed mother bring up a flock of brothers and sisters, and she seemed much older than her age and more mature. She was hard-working, obedient, pure, self-controlled, and full of faith. Those were the virtues that were to lead to her magnificent sacrifice. When a young ruffian of eighteen tried to draw her into sin, she naturally, as a Christian, refused; then he, in fury, killed her with his dagger. Maria Goretti died simply out of obedience to the commandments she had learned in her catechism. Yet she was only a little peasant girl who could not read, and she was not yet twelve years old.

∞

"Let the little children come to me, for of such is the kingdom of God . . . Unless you become as children, you shall not enter into Heaven." We read these words of our Lord at the beginning of this book. Are they not clearer now? Does not the example of these young saints give us a better understanding of Jesus' words?

Christ calls children to Himself in a very special way. Childhood is the age of generosity. Of course, all children have their faults, their weaknesses, their sins — this they know well enough. But they do not yet have the responsibilities of the grown man or woman. They are freer to throw themselves into a great cause, to follow a great example. Christ is calling you to be like Him — that is, to cultivate in yourselves what you know is the best that is in you — kindness, courage, perseverance, charity toward others, faith and trust in God. And isn't it true that you feel happiest when you are taking a little trouble to get closer to our Lord, our only model?

What did the Master mean, as He taught the crowds on the hills of Galilee and the shores of Lake Tiberias, when He urged His listeners to "become as children"? He meant this: For the little child, everything is simple and easy. He has no bad thoughts; he loves those who surround him; he is trusting; he knows nothing about evil.

Childhood, then, is a time of marvelous innocence. Unfortunately, that innocence does not last, and for most of us, the time comes soon enough for temptations, faults, lies, disobedience, sin. By urging His followers to become as little children, our Lord did not mean that children were perfect, but that we were to try to return to that spirit of innocence, of hope, of trust in God that we had in those happy days when we knew no evil.

The saints whose stories we have read here did nothing else than remain faithful, all through their lives, to that command. Some, as we have seen, died in their youth. Others lived to a ripe old age, but they retained their "spirit of childhood"; they continued to love Jesus as they had in their youth, and their Christian hearts, at sixty, were as young as when they made their First Communion.

This, then, is what these examples teach us. No one of us knows whether God will call us to Himself after a few years or after a long life of effort, of sorrows, and of joys; that does not depend on us. What does depend on us is that we should remain young of heart and soul, however short or long our lives.

"Let the Little Children Come to Me"

So may I give this very simple advice to all of you, my unknown friends, who read these lines: Always remain faithful to your youth — that is, to everything generous and courageous in you, everything that places the best things first in your souls. That is the price of true happiness on earth — and of the Kingdom which has been promised you.

Henri Daniel-Rops

(1901-1965)

The much-beloved Catholic historian and author Henri Daniel-Rops was born Henri Jules Charles Petiot in France in 1901. The grandson of peasants and the son of an artillery officer, he showed early in life the brilliance and intellectual dynamism that would bring him worldwide renown as a writer: before he was twenty-one, he had earned the equivalent of Master's degrees in law, geography, and history. He became a teacher, but quickly showed that his first love — and his greatest talent — was writing. His first book, *Our Anxiety*, was published in 1926 under the *nom de plume* Henri Daniel-Rops, which he continued to use to the end of his life.

By this time Daniel-Rops, raised a Catholic, had fallen away from the Church and become an agnostic. *Our Anxiety* reflects his spiritual restlessness. By the 1930s, however, he had made his way back to the Catholic Faith. He found, according to his biographer Justine Krug Boisson, that "only in Jesus Christ could the technological age be reconciled with the spiritual needs of man."

Already an accomplished historian, Daniel-Rops became fascinated with the workings of God in history. His writings began to reflect this preoccupation. He wrote a history of the Jews before

Golden Legend of Young Saints

Christ (*Sacred History*), an account of the apostolic Church (*The Church of the Apostles and Martyrs*), and *A History of the Church of Christ*. Many regard his book *Jesus and His Times* as his greatest achievement. It was a huge bestseller in France, catapulting this energetic historian to worldwide renown and winning his books attention from Catholics and non-Catholics alike.

In addition to teaching, lecturing, and writing, Daniel-Rops was director of the French publishing house Fayard, as well as the popular religious magazine *Ecclesia*. He still found time to write more than seventy religious books: novels, historical studies, poetry, and children's stories. He was also editor-in-chief of the massive 150-volume *Twentieth-Century Encyclopedia of Catholicism*.

His writings brought Daniel-Rops many honors. He was elected the youngest member of the French Academy in 1955, and the following year, Pope Pius XII awarded him the Cross of the Order of St. Gregory the Great. He was greatly respected for his ability to express ancient spiritual truths with a new freshness and a journalist's sense of immediacy. In addition, the strong Catholic faith with which he wrote allows readers to draw from his works not only the historical context of the great events of the Church, but also a fervent reaffirmation of the love and providence of God.

∞

Sophia Institute Press®

Sophia Institute® is a nonprofit institution that seeks to restore man's knowledge of eternal truth, including man's knowledge of his own nature, his relation to other persons, and his relation to God. Sophia Institute Press® serves this end in numerous ways: it publishes translations of foreign works to make them accessible for the first time to English-speaking readers; it brings out-of-print books back into print; and it publishes important new books that fulfill the ideals of Sophia Institute®. These books afford readers a rich source of the enduring wisdom of mankind.

Sophia Institute Press® makes these high-quality books available to the general public by using advanced technology and by soliciting donations to subsidize its general publishing costs. Your generosity can help Sophia Institute Press® to provide the public with editions of works containing the enduring wisdom of the ages. Please send your tax-deductible contribution to the address below. We welcome your questions, comments, and suggestions.

For your free catalog, call:
Toll-free: 1-800-888-9344

or write:
Sophia Institute Press® ♦ Box 5284 ♦ Manchester, NH 03108